Ron Carter's Comprehensive Bass Method
- new edition   - advanced level

Copyright © 2015 Ron Carter

Retrac Productions, Inc.
New York, NY, USA
Photographs: Fortuna Sung

www.roncarterjazz.com

Printed in the USA

1. Don't try this at home!

2. Proper position of the left hand. Note that the thumb is under the second finger.

Pizzicato

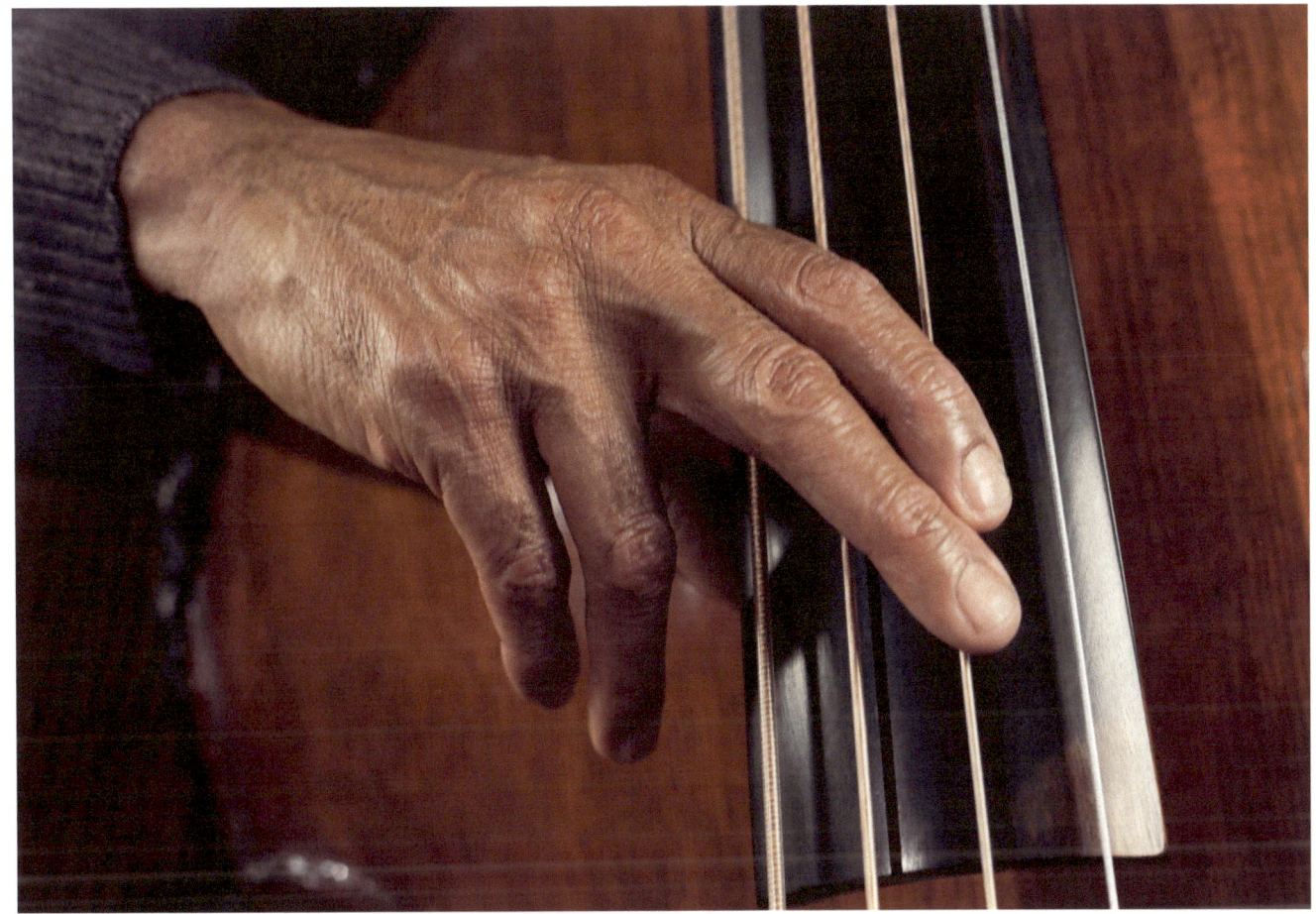

3. Proper placement and position of right hand for pizzicato

One of the problems facing the young bassist is that of producing a good pizzicato sound - one that produces a true tone, and one whose "delay time" (the length of note resonance) can be controlled by the player.

the photo above shows the proper position of the right hand (pizzicato hand).

When playing pizzicato, the bassist should think in terms of the right hand "slurring" the notes (as if using the bow) when crossing the strings, from the G string to the D string, the D string to the A string, and the A string to the E string. When going from a lower string to a higher string, the same principle applies.

4. Proper position of the instrument when standing

Contents

Pages 13, 26, 30 and 32 include QR codes
with links to video demos by Ron Carter

Explanation of Symbols	1
½ Position	2
1st Position	4
2nd Position	8
2½ Position	11
3rd Position	16
3½ Position	20
4th Position	24
4½ Position	29
5th Position	33
5½ Position	38
Etudes	41
Scales	46
Horizontal Technique	52
Arpeggios	53
Blues in the Closet (Ron Carter bass solo)	60
For Toddlers Only	62
Receipt, Please	63
Playing Tip 1: Tips for Players	64
Playing Tip 2: Improvisation	65
Biography, Awards, Library	66

Explanation of Symbols

0 open string

1 first finger

2 second finger

4 fourth finger

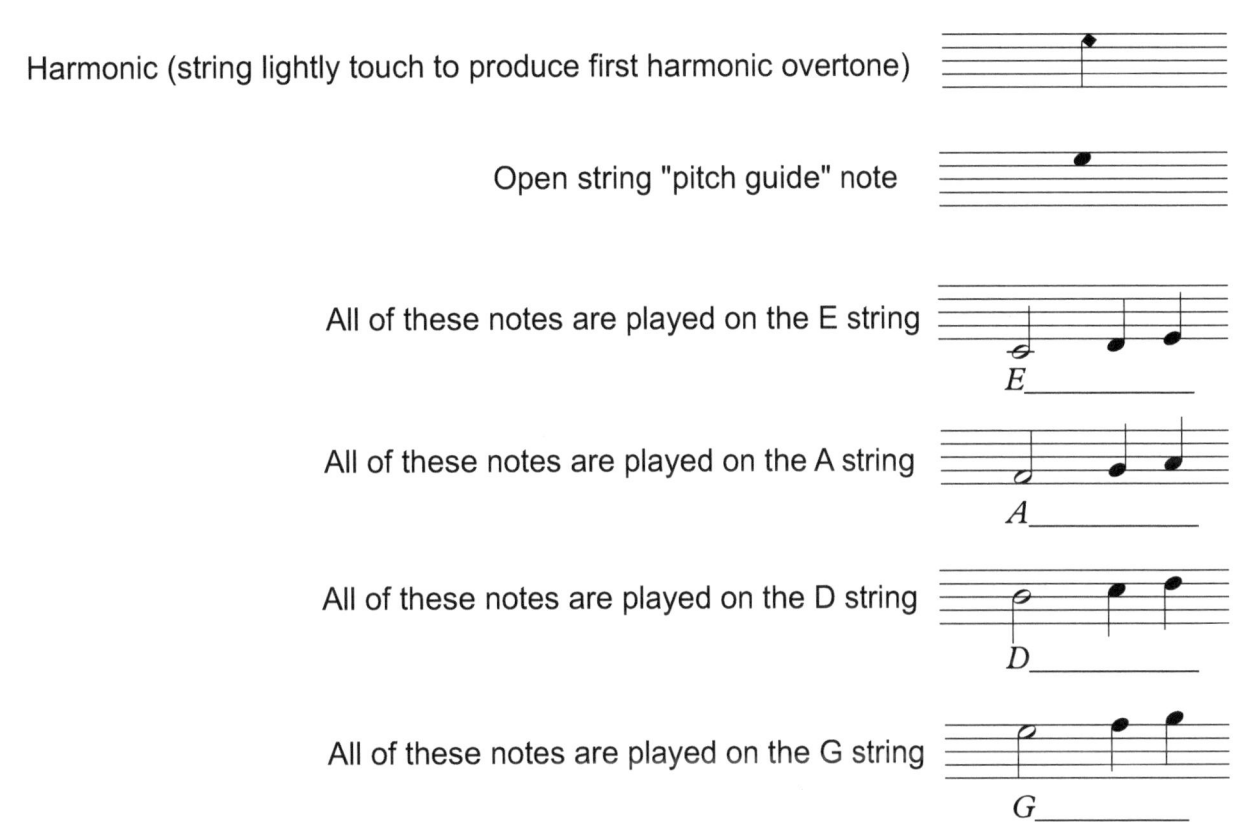

Harmonic (string lightly touch to produce first harmonic overtone)

Open string "pitch guide" note

All of these notes are played on the E string

All of these notes are played on the A string

All of these notes are played on the D string

All of these notes are played on the G string

♯ Sharp (note as printed is raised ½ step)

♭ Flat (note as printed is lowered ½ step)

♮ Natural (note that has been raised or lowered is returned to the note as shown in key signature)

× Double sharp (note is raised whole step)

𝅝 A whole note that gets four counts

𝅗𝅥 A half note that gets two counts

𝅘𝅥 A quarter note that gets one count

𝅘𝅥𝅮 An eighth note that get half of quarter note value

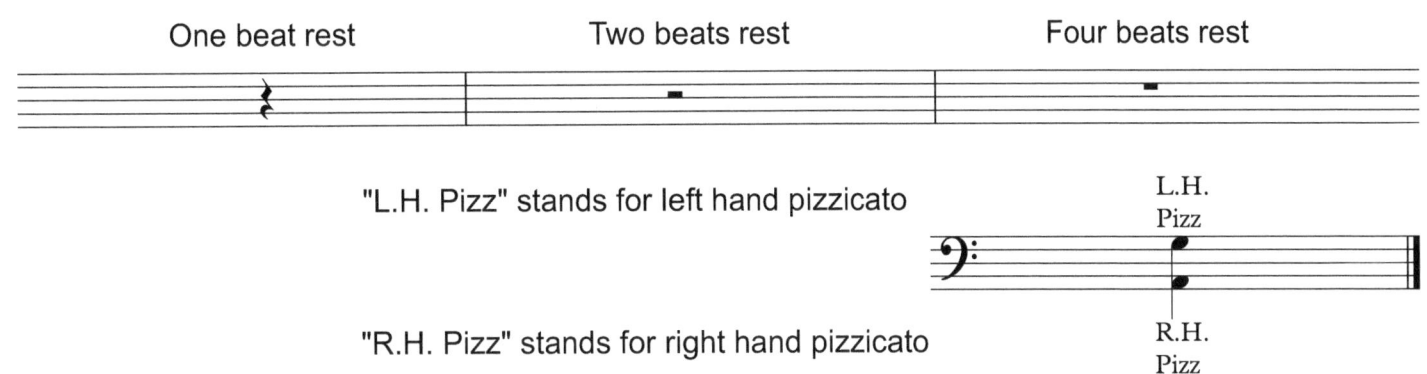

One beat rest

Two beats rest

Four beats rest

"L.H. Pizz" stands for left hand pizzicato

"R.H. Pizz" stands for right hand pizzicato

½ Position

In the picture (see **2**) you will notice that all the fingers are curved and the balls of the finger tips are placed on the string.

In this position you will notice that the 2nd finger should match the pitch of the A string as in the diagram.

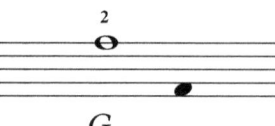

The same "pitch guide" note holds true for 2nd finger on the D string to open E string.

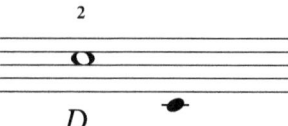

On the E string, the "pitch guide" note is 4th finger G to open G string.

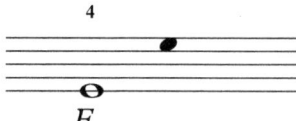

The notes and fingering in this position are:

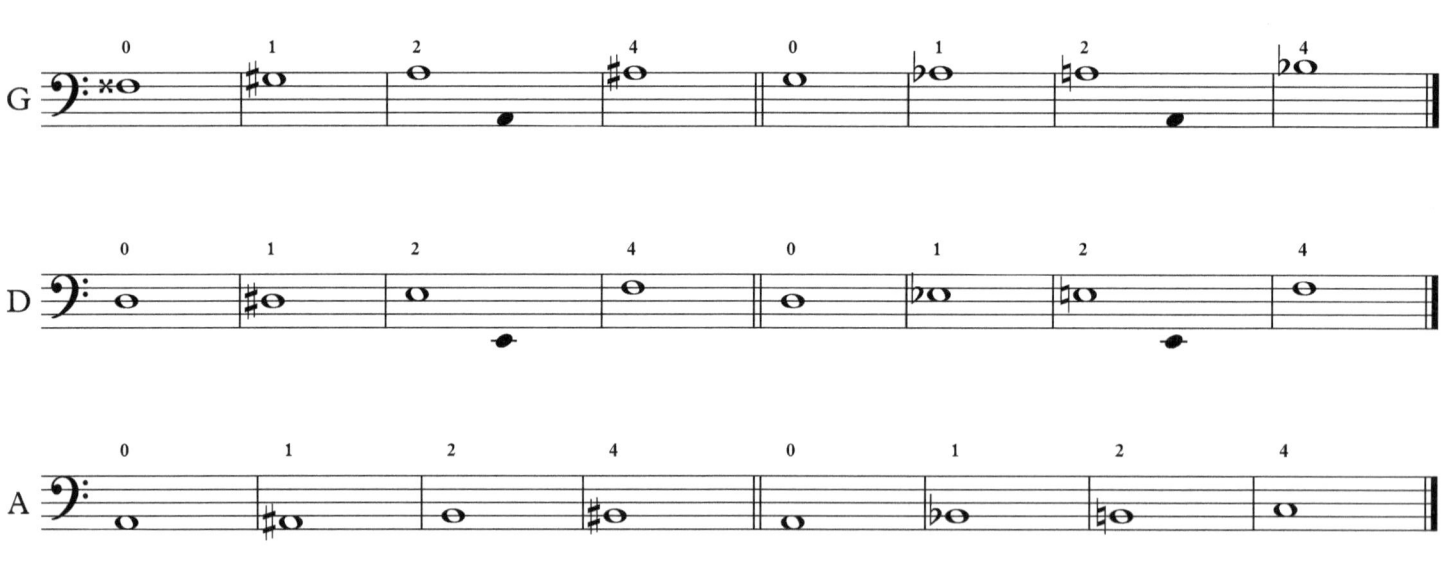

1st Position

This position is ½ step higher than the previous position. The "pitch guide" notes are:

on the G string, 1st finger A to open A string;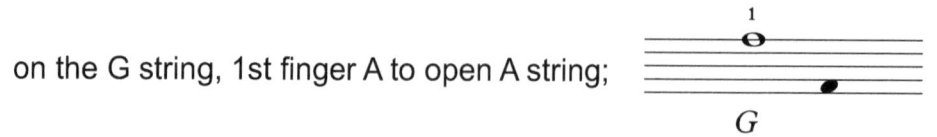

on the D string, 1st finger E to open E string;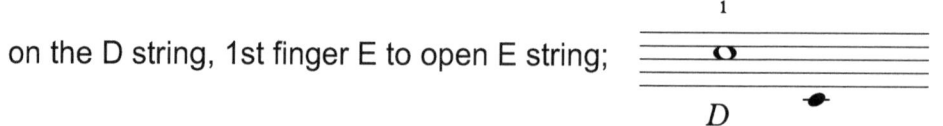

on the E string, 2nd finger G to open G string.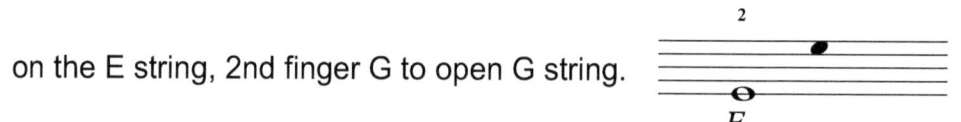

The notes and fingering in this position are:

1st Position
Exercises

Etudes
Positions ½ and 1

I.

Etudes - Positions ½ and 1

II.

2nd Position

This position is ½ step higher than the previous position. The "pitch guide" notes are:

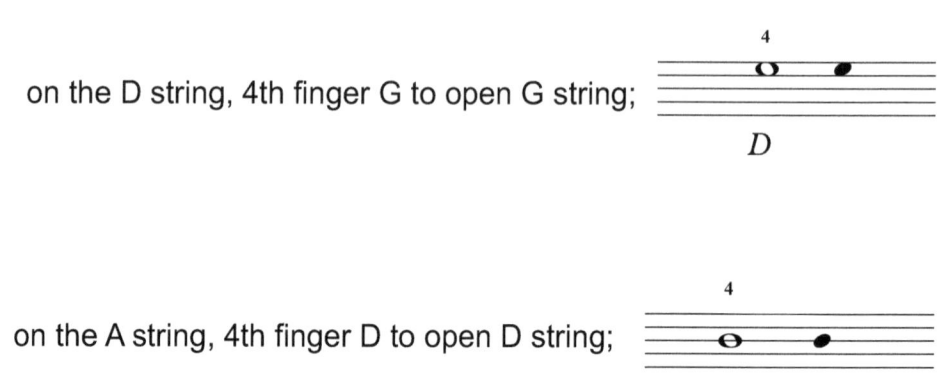

on the D string, 4th finger G to open G string;

on the A string, 4th finger D to open D string;

on the E string, 4th finger A to open A string;

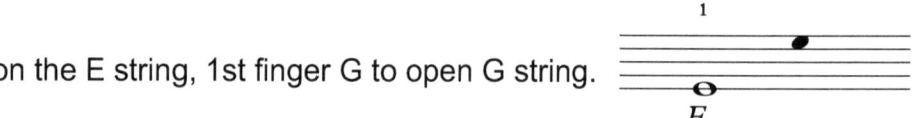

on the E string, 1st finger G to open G string.

The notes and fingering in this position are:

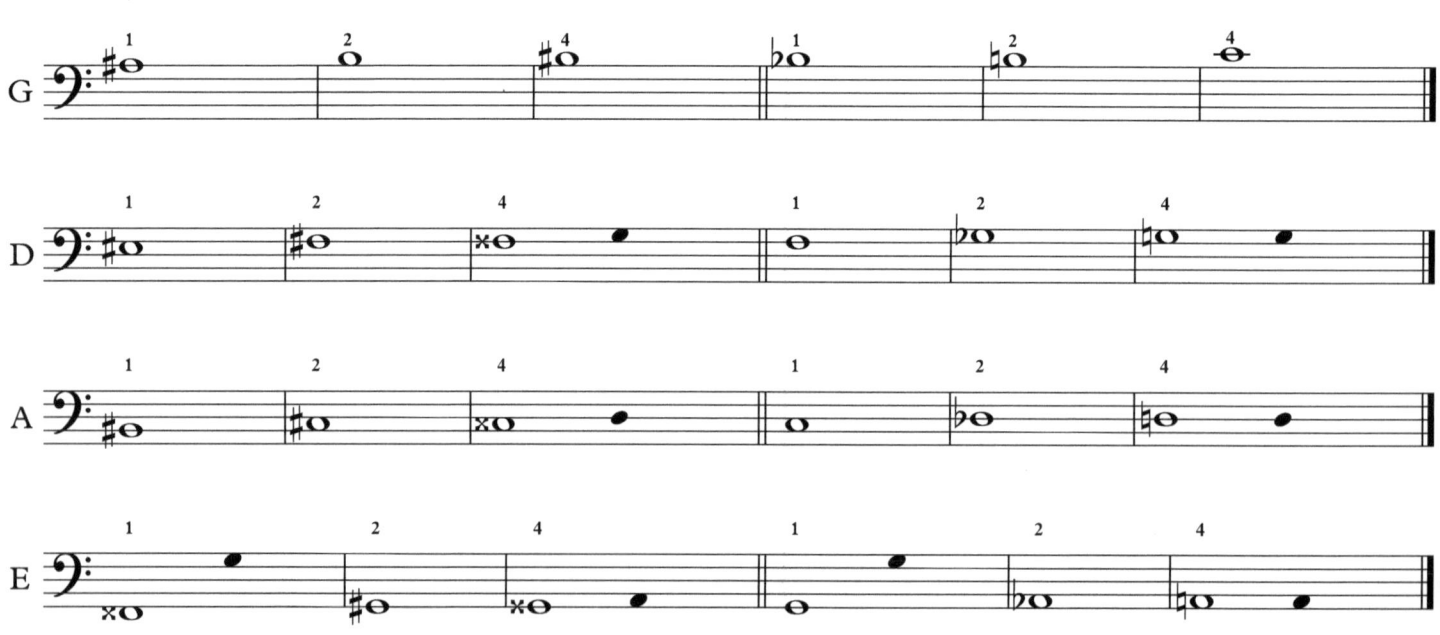

Etudes
Positions ½ through 2

2½ Position

This position is ½ step higher than the previous position. The "pitch guide" notes are:

on the D string, 2nd finger G to open G string;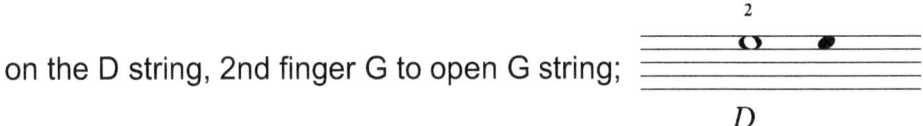

on the A string, 2nd finger D to open D string;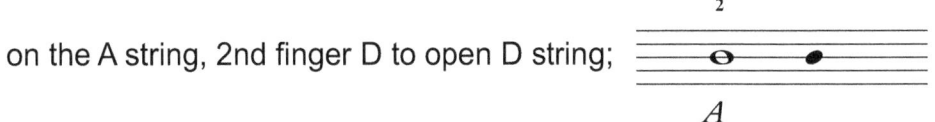

on the E string, 2nd finger A to open A string.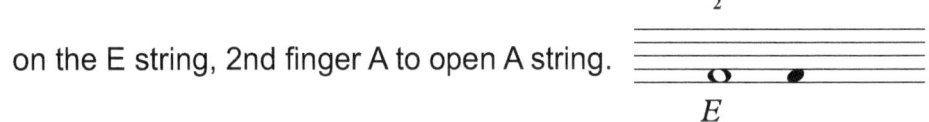

The notes and fingering in this position are:

2½ Position
Exercises

I.

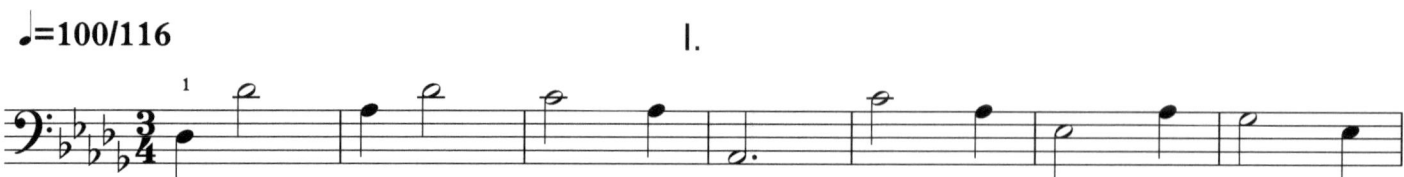

II.

2½ Position
Exercises

Etudes
Positions ½ through 2½

I.

Etudes - Positions ½ through 2½

II.

3rd Position

This position is ½ step higher than the previous position. The "pitch guide" notes are:

on the G string, 4th finger D to open D string;

on the D string, 4th finger A to open A string;

on the D string, 1st finger G to open G string;

on the A string, 4th finger E to open E string;

on the A string, 1st finger D to open D string;

on the E string, 1st finger A to open A string.

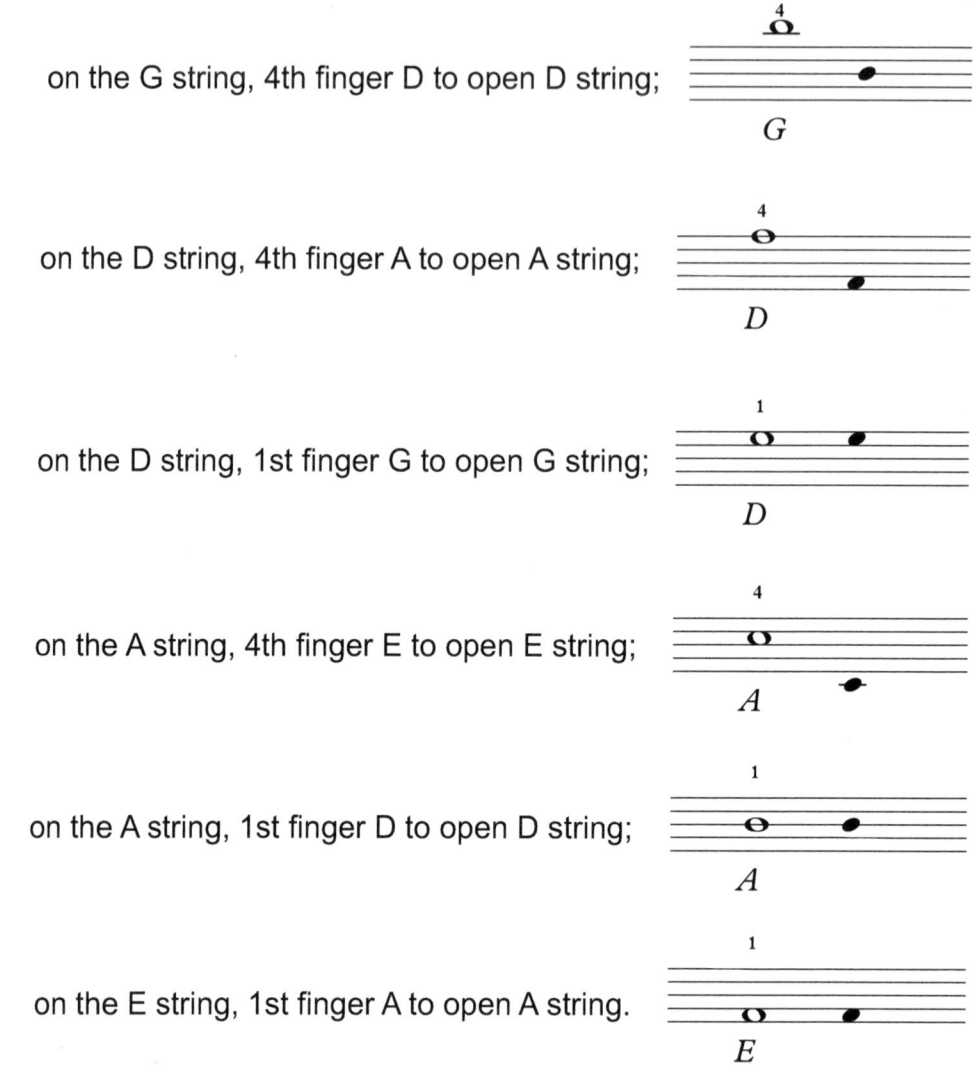

The notes and fingering in this position are:

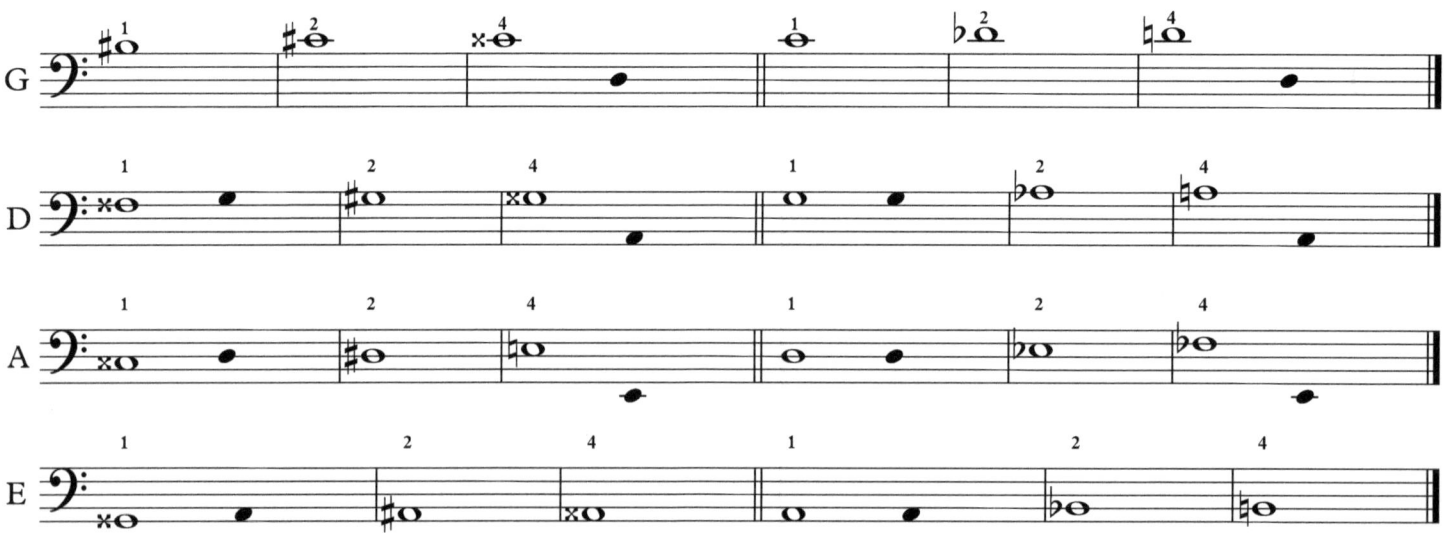

Etudes
Positions ½ through 3

I.

Etudes - Positions ½ through 3

II.

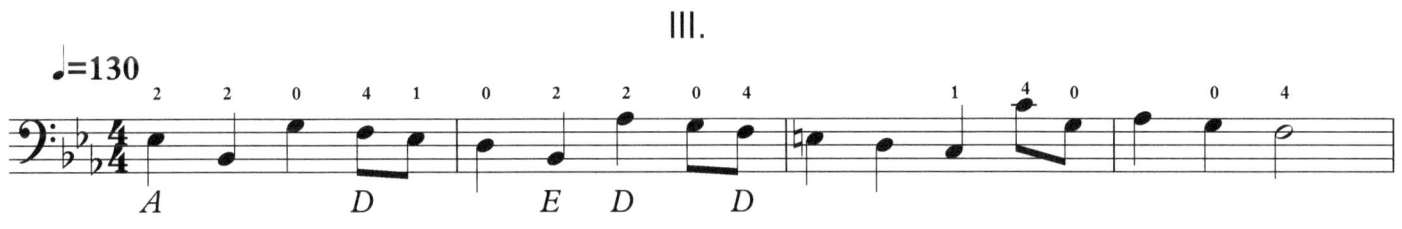

III.

3½ Position

This position is ½ step higher than the previous position. The "pitch guide" notes are:

on the G string, 2nd finger D to open D string;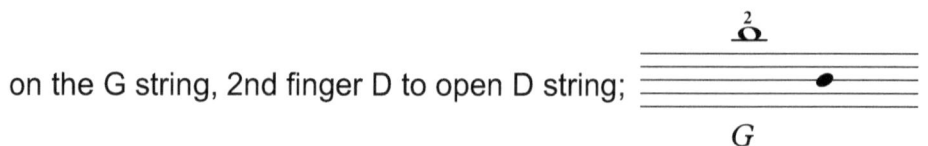

on the D string, 2nd finger A to open A string;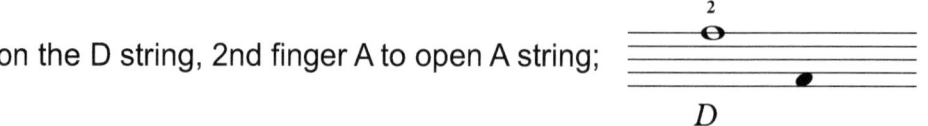

on the A string, 2nd finger E to open E string.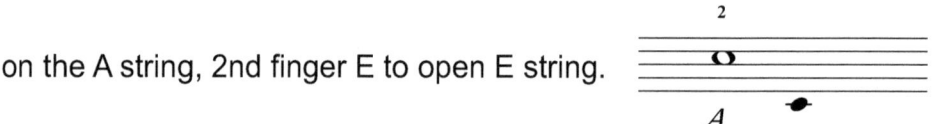

The notes and fingering in this position are:

3½ Position
Exercises

Etudes
Positions ½ through 3½

4th Position

This position is ½ step higher than the previous position. The "pitch guide" notes are:

on the G string, 4th finger E to open E string;

on the G string, 1st finger D to open D string;

on the D string, 1st finger A to open A string;

on the A string, 1st finger E to open E string.

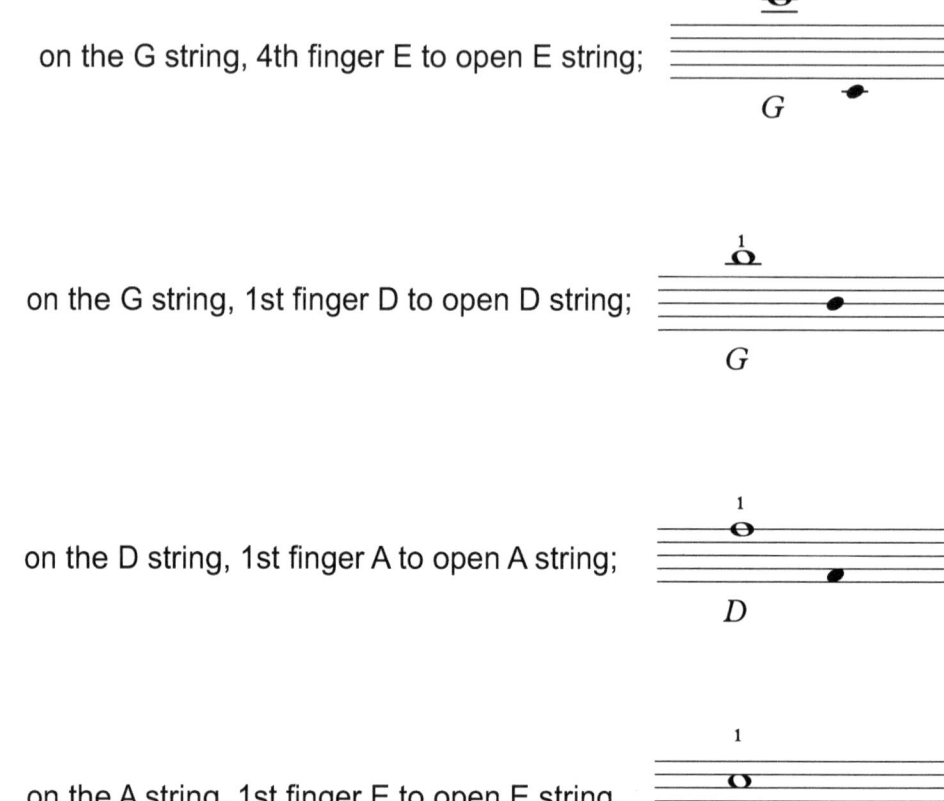

The notes and fingering in this position are:

4th Position
Exercises

I.
♩=100

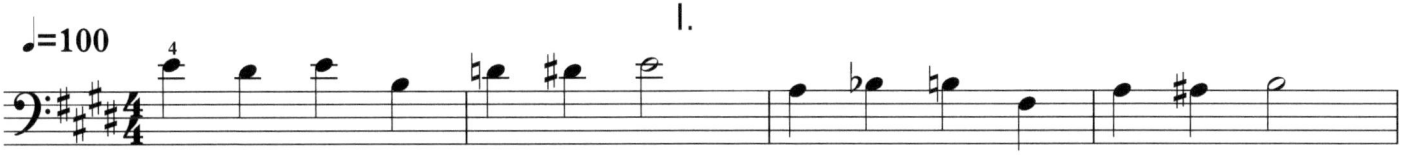

II.
♩=116

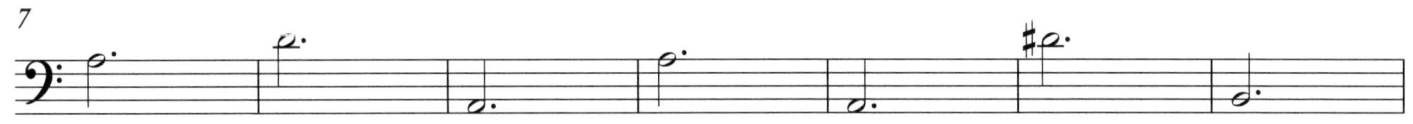

4th Position
Exercises

III.

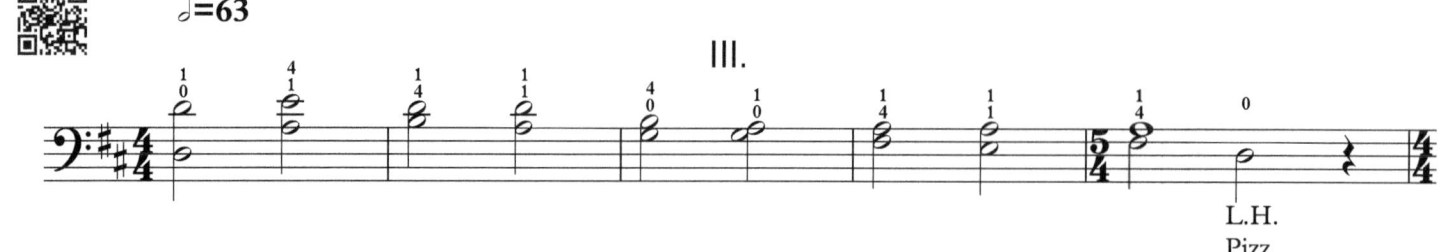
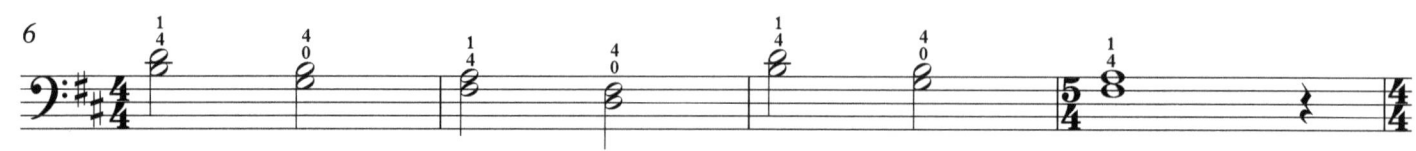
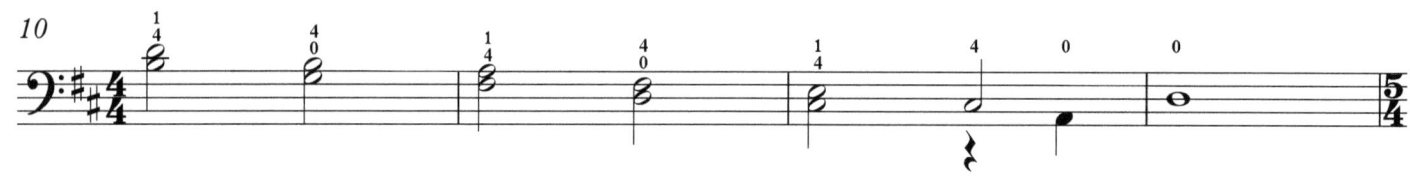
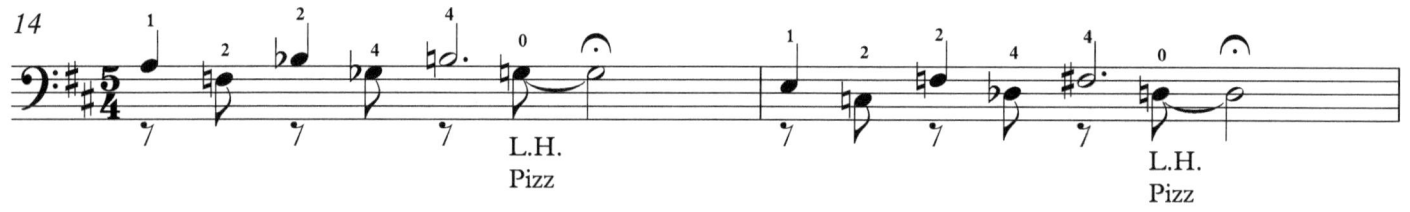
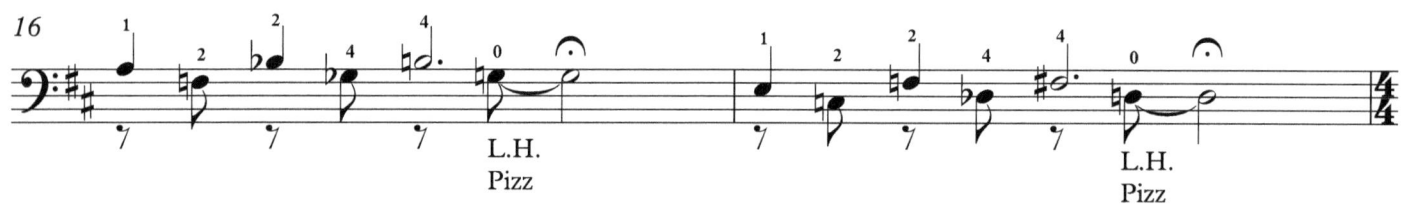
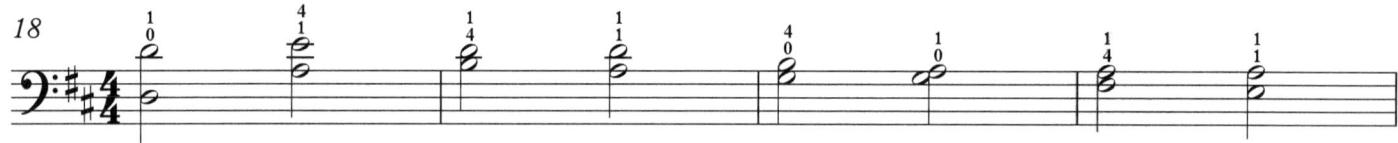
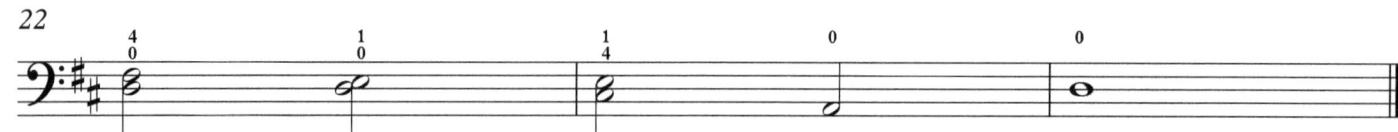

Etudes
Positions ½ through 4

I.

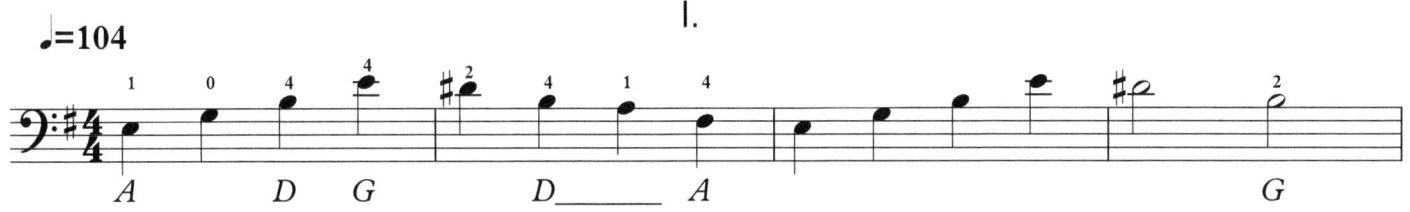

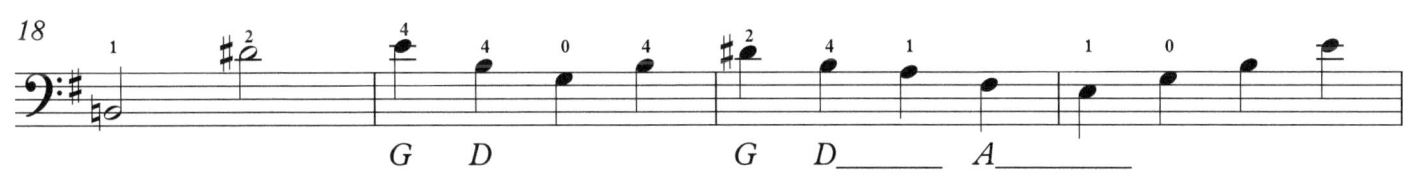

Etudes - Positions ½ through 4

II.

4½ Position

This position is ½ step higher than the previous position. The "pitch guide" notes are:

on the G string, 2nd finger E to open E string;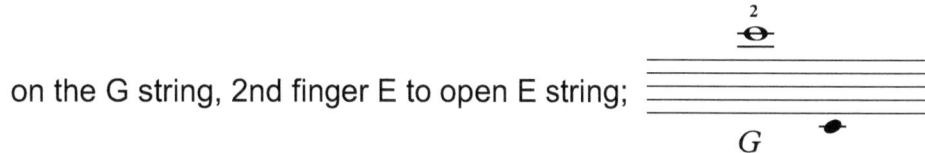

on the A string, 4th finger G to open G string;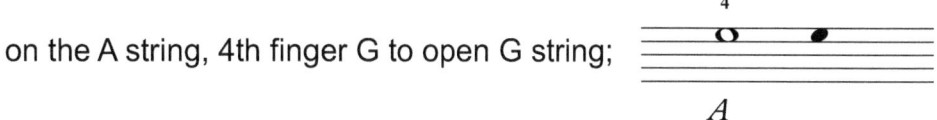

on the E string, 4th finger D to open D string.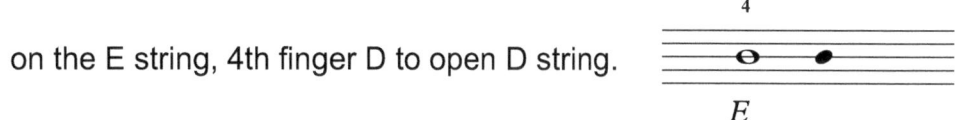

The notes and fingering in this position are:

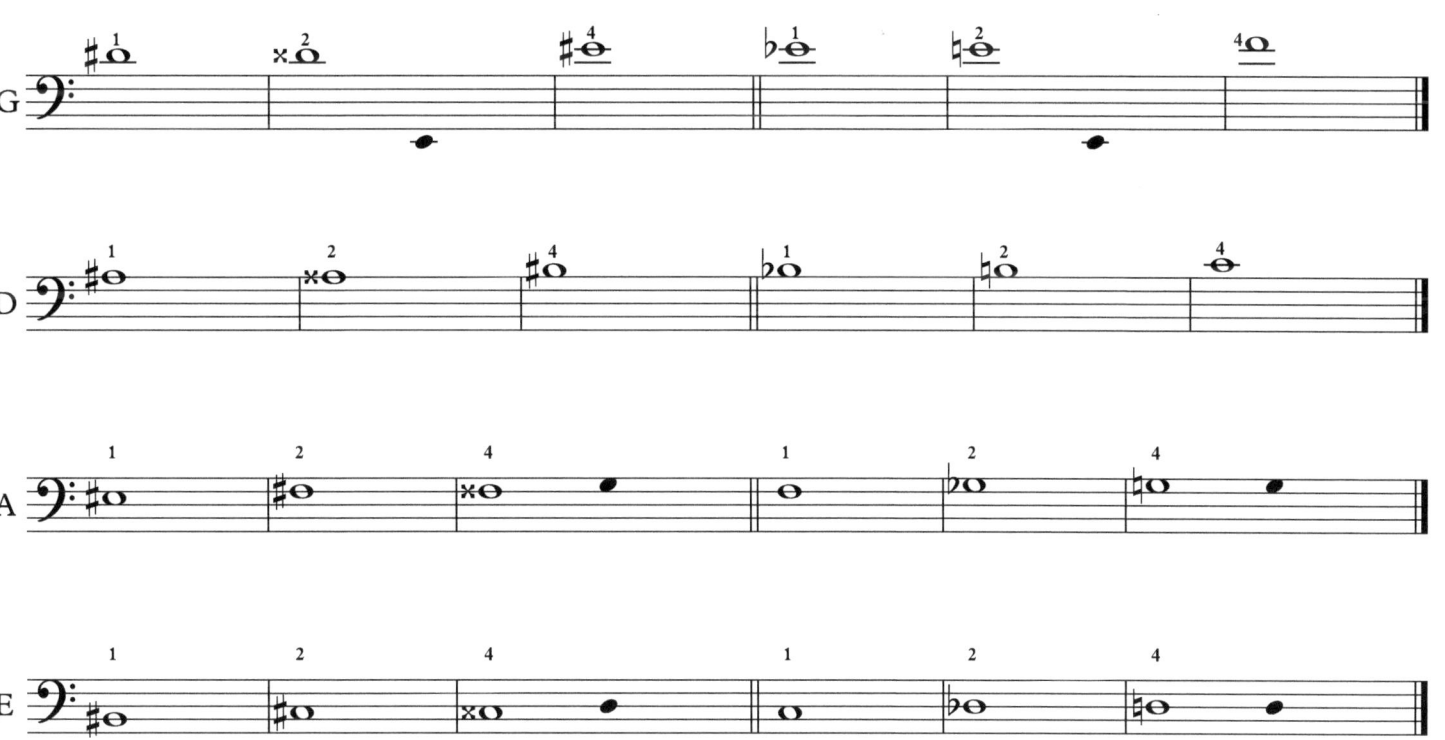

4½ Position
Exercises

* Extend 1st finger to play harmonic

Etudes
Positions ½ through 4½

I.

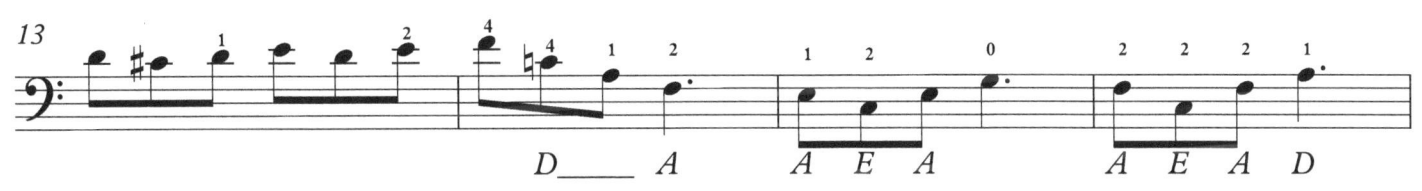

Etudes - Positions ½ through 4½

II.

5th Position

This position is ½ step higher than the previous position. The "pitch guide" notes are:

on the G string, 1st finger E to open E string;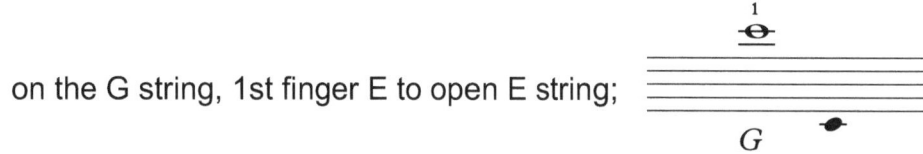

on the A string, 2nd finger G to open G string;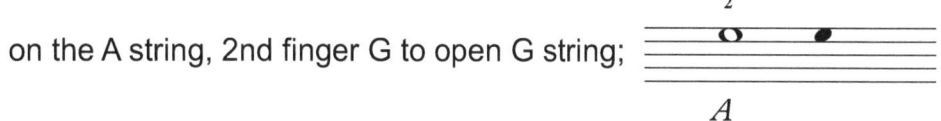

on the E string, 2nd finger D to open D string.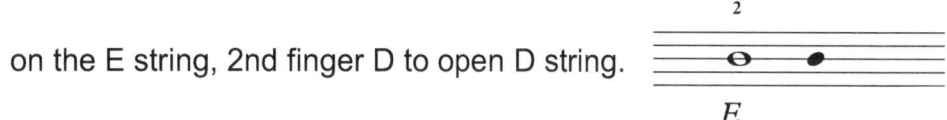

The notes and fingering in this position are:

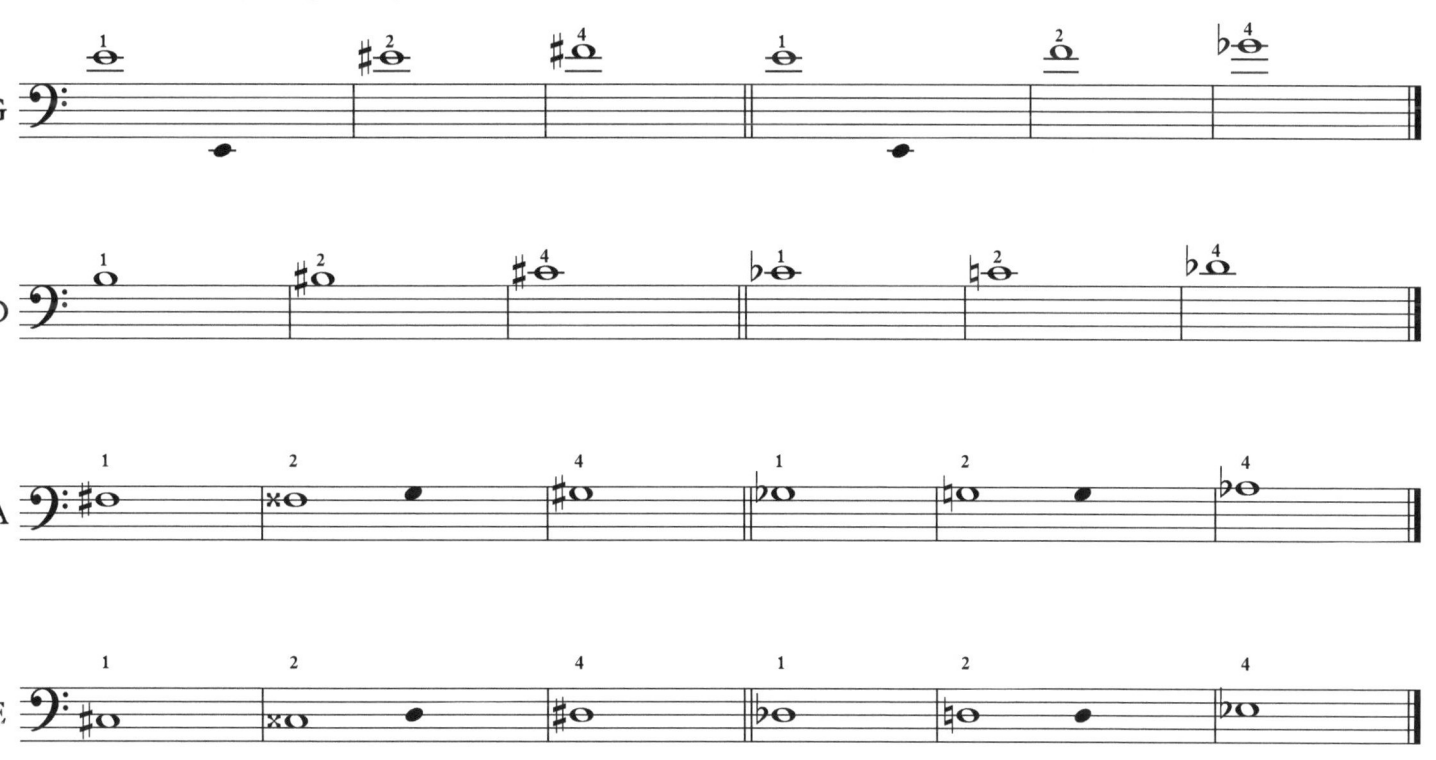

5th Position
Exercises

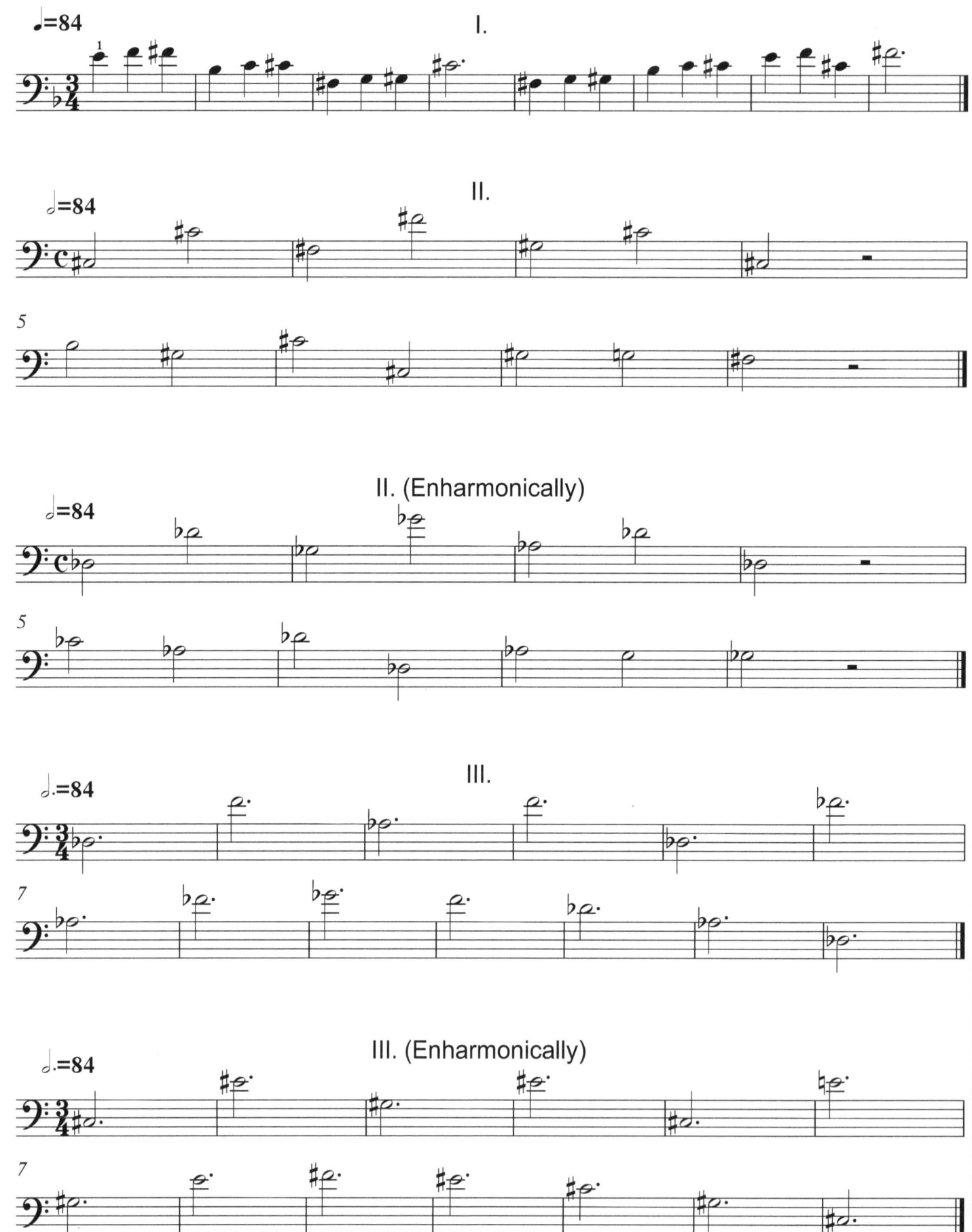

Etudes
Positions ½ through 5

5½ Position

This position is ½ step higher than the previous position. However, the 3rd finger is often used in place of the 4th finger.

In this position the player has the option to press the string down at the octave or merely touch the string with only the 3rd finger, thus producing a harmonic.

It is also in this position that the thumb leaves its place under the neck, and now moves to the side of the neck.

The "pitch guide" notes for this position are:

on the A string, 1st finger G to open G string;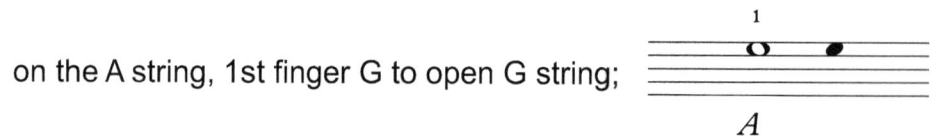

on the E string, 1st finger D to open D string;

The notes and fingering in this position are:

5½ Position
Exercises

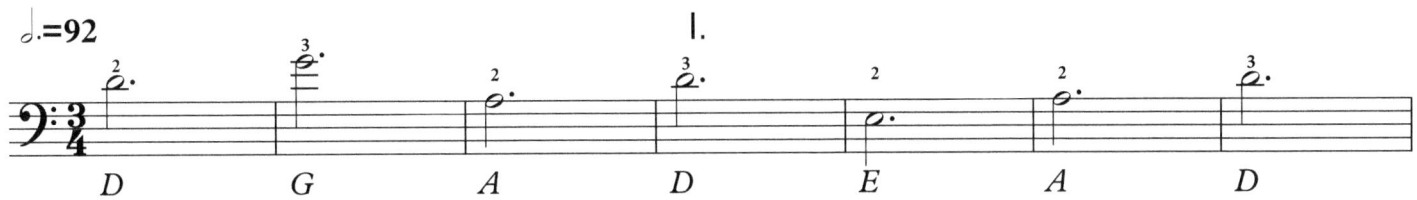
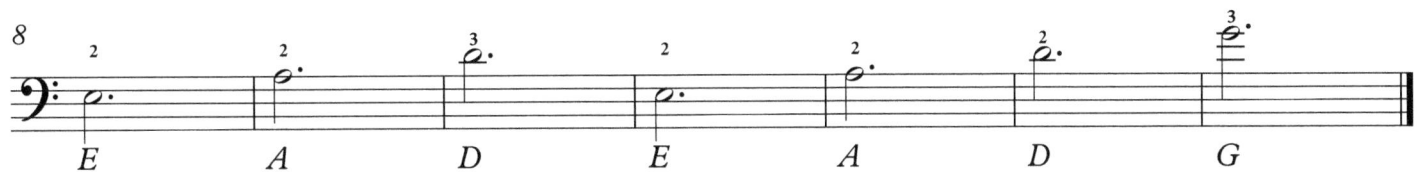

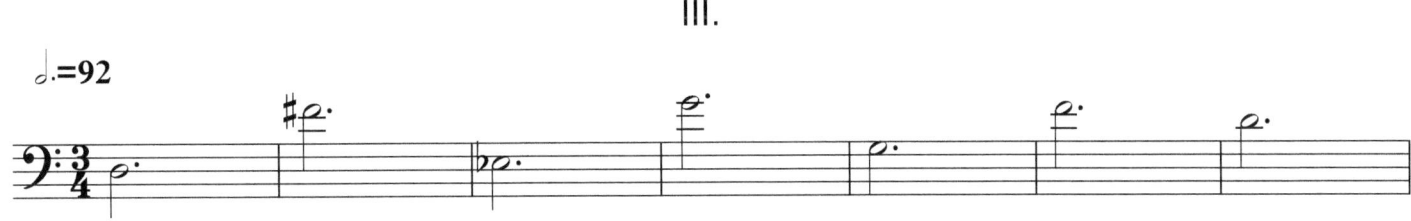

Etudes
Positions ½ through 5½

Etudes

The following etudes serve as supplemental material for the student for these purposes:

1. To devise his or her own fingering.
2. To see how quickly fingering can be accomplished.
3. And to expose him or her to different harmonies, with both chords and scales.

Remember to strive for good tone, a long "delay time" (the length of note resonance), and a good feel for this approach to produce an outstanding sound from the instrument.

I.

Etudes

II.

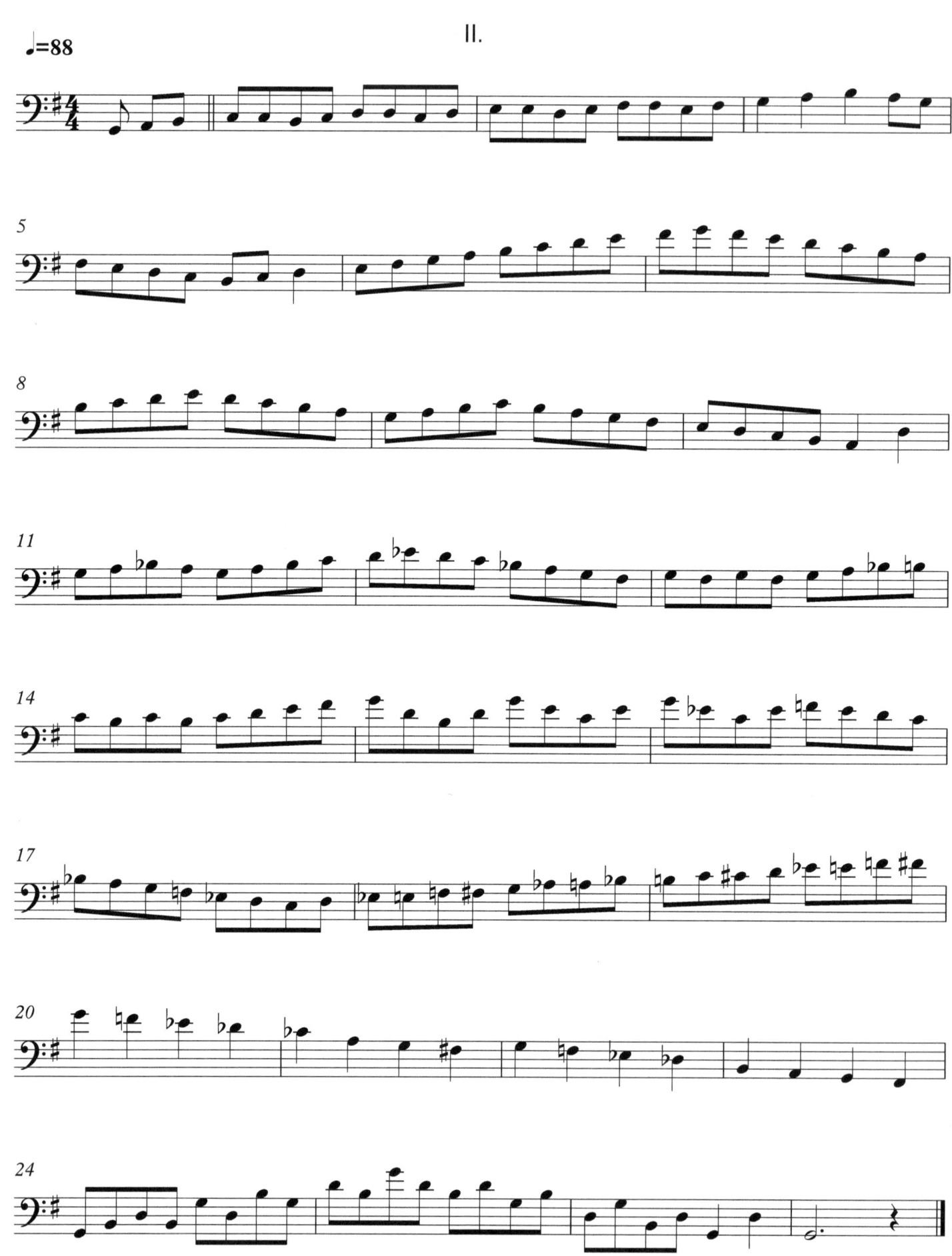

Etudes

III.

Etudes

V.

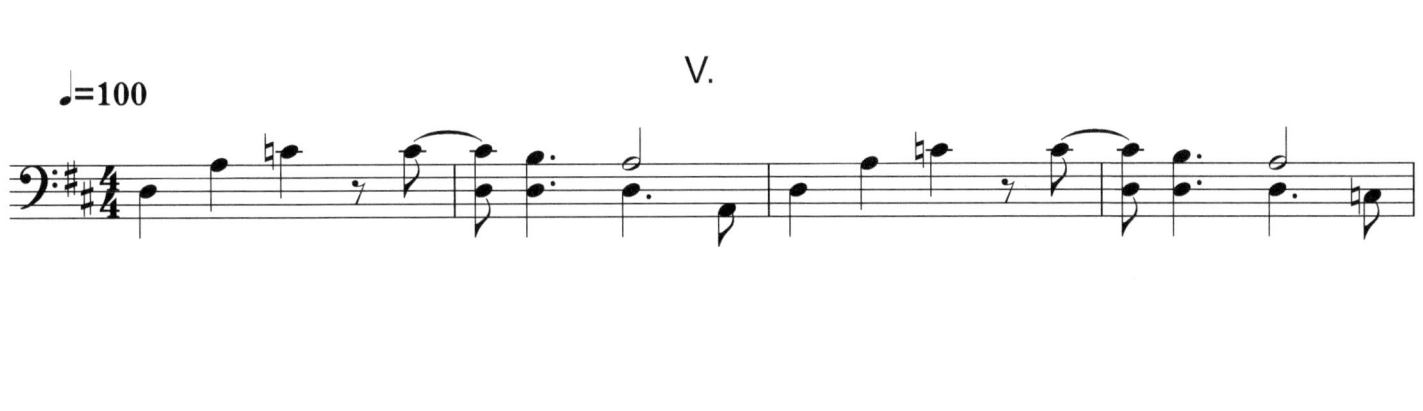

Repeat last 4 bars ad lib, then fade

Scales

The following set of scales is to be practiced daily, first at a slow tempo then gradually increasing the speed. I recommend the routine below whenever scales are practiced for continued development of pitch, tone, and technique.

C Major

OR

F Major

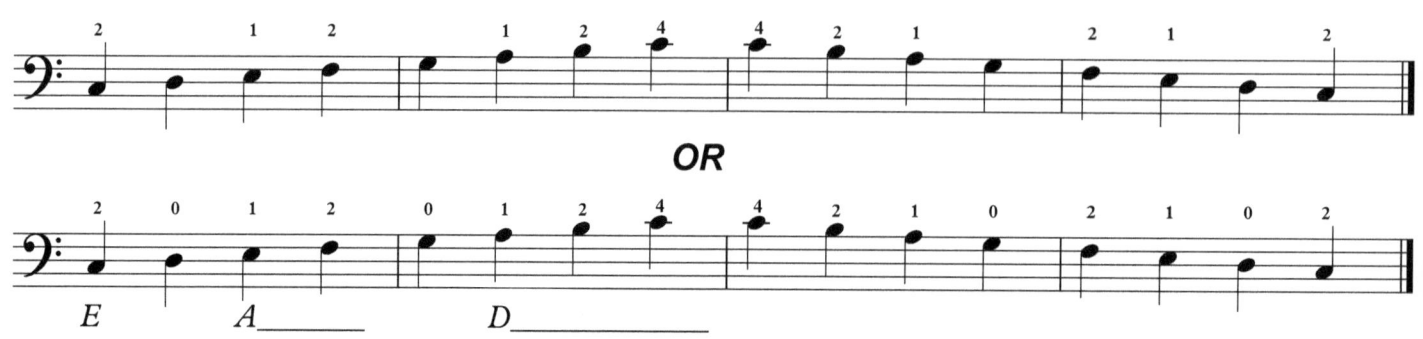

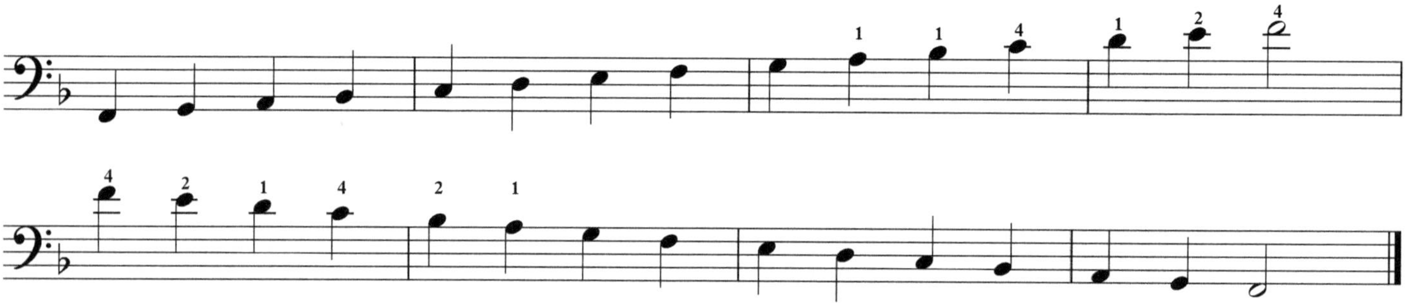

OR

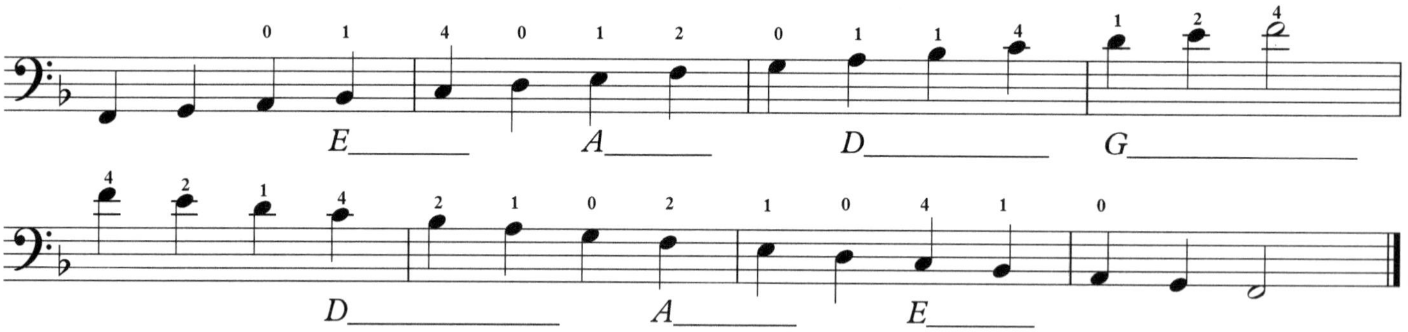

OR

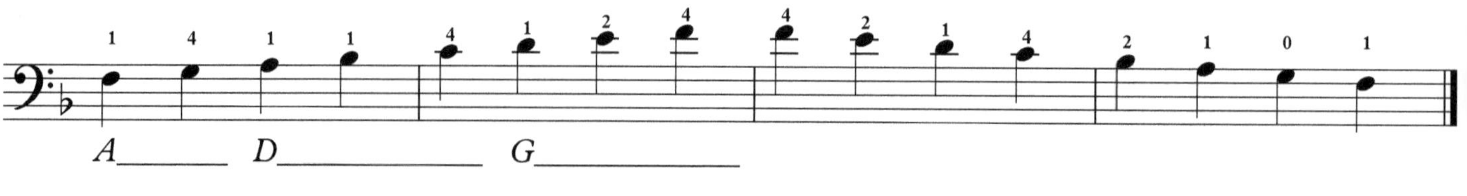

B♭ Major

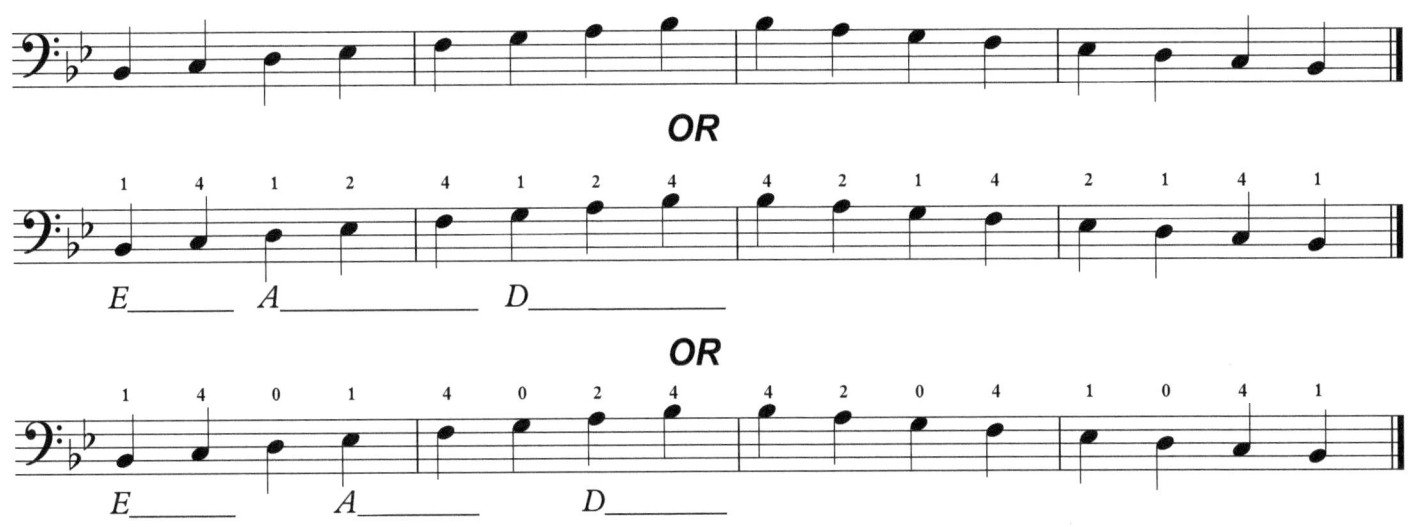

E♭ Major

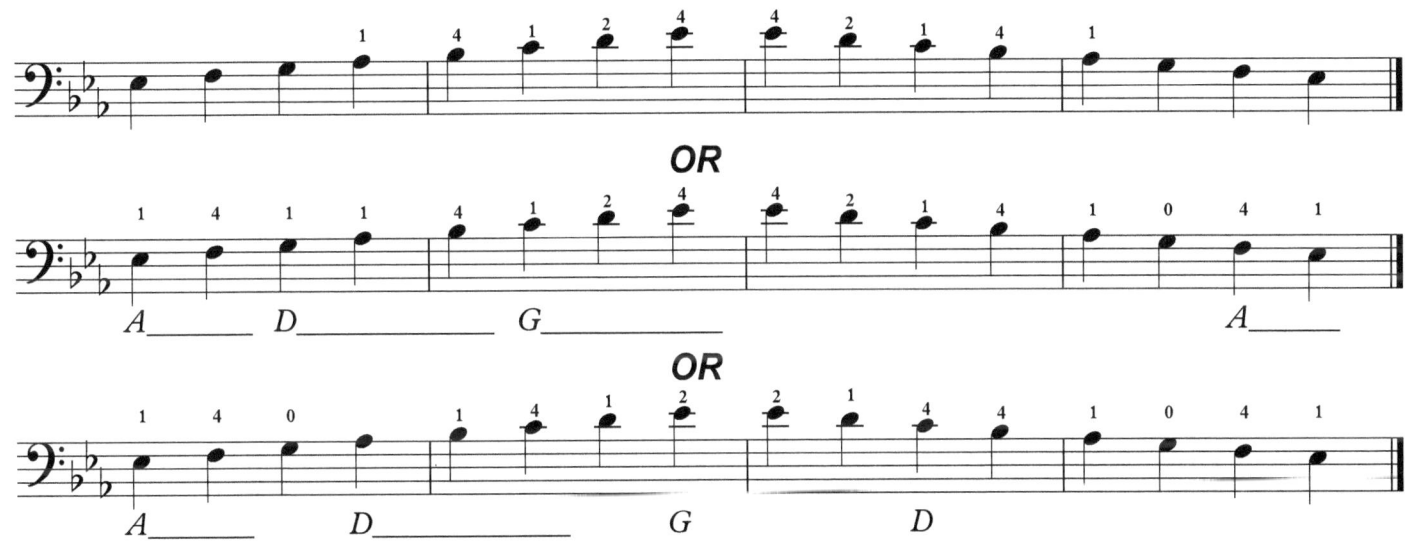

A♭ Major

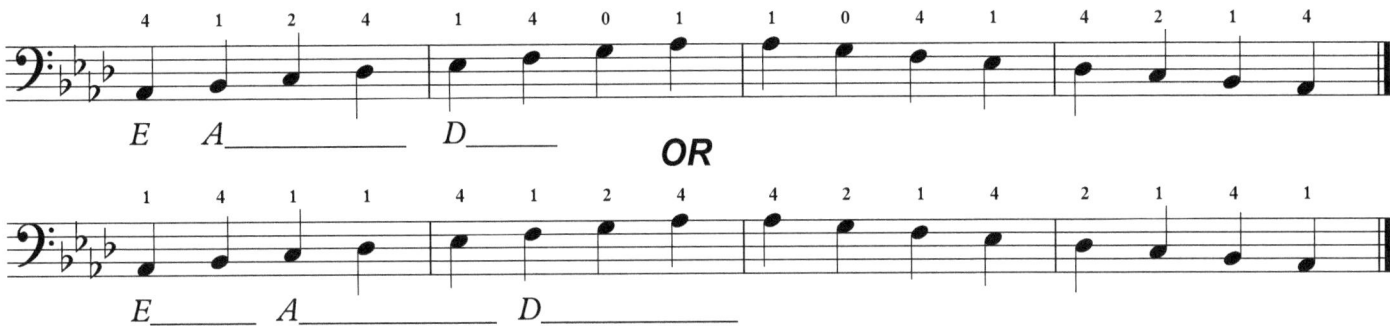

D♭ Major

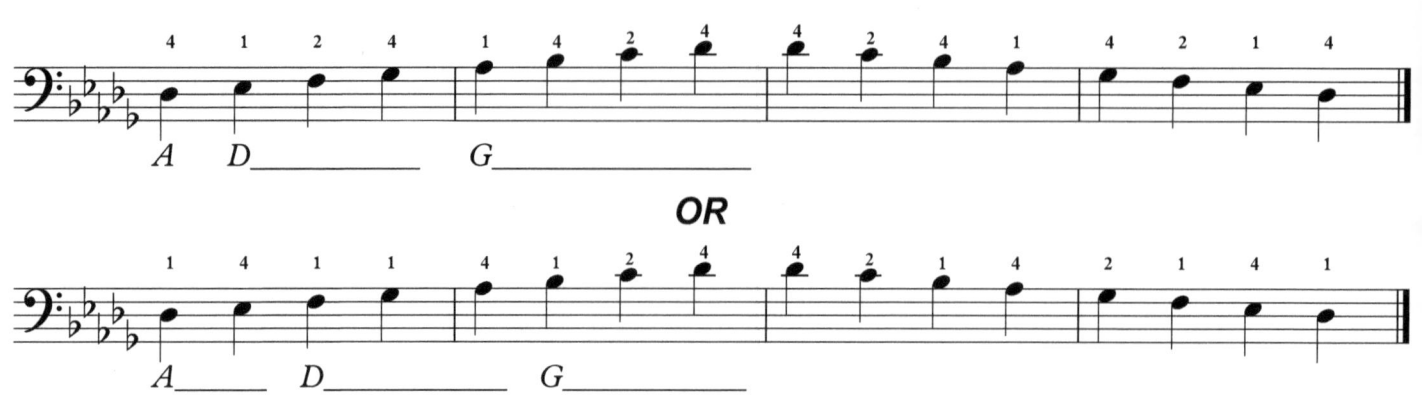

G♭ Major

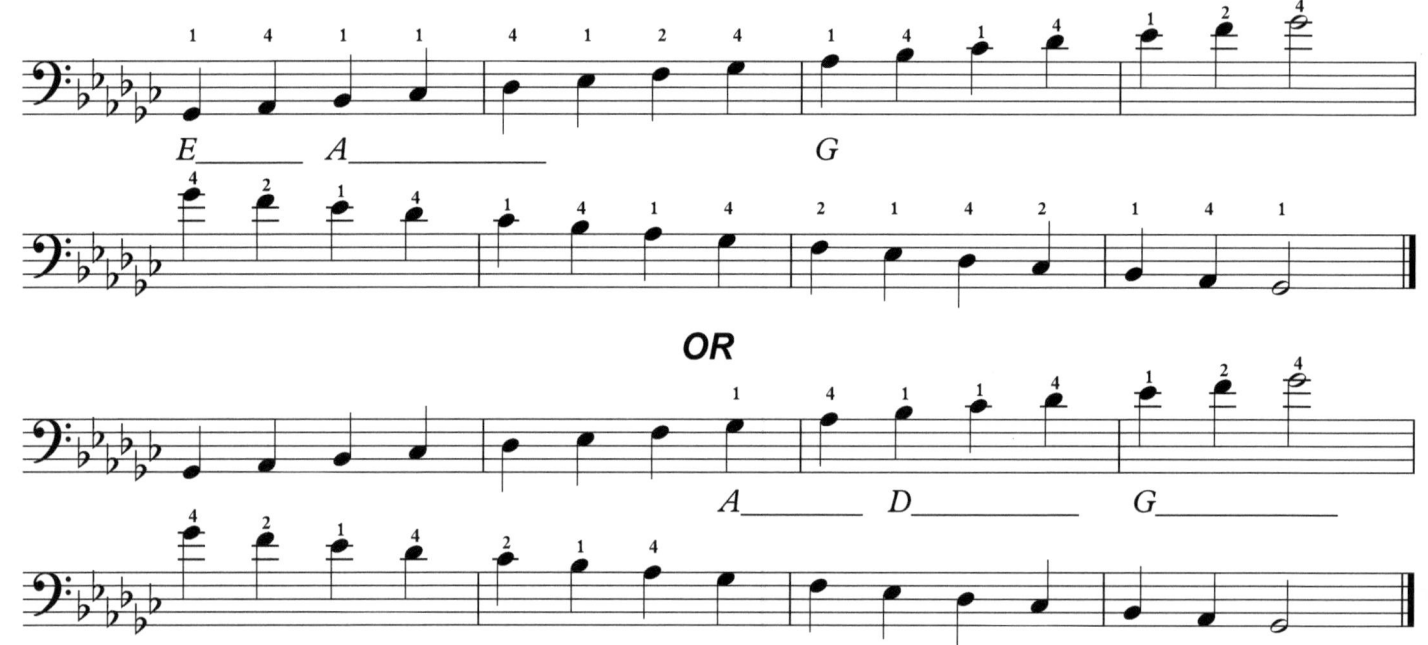

C♭ Major

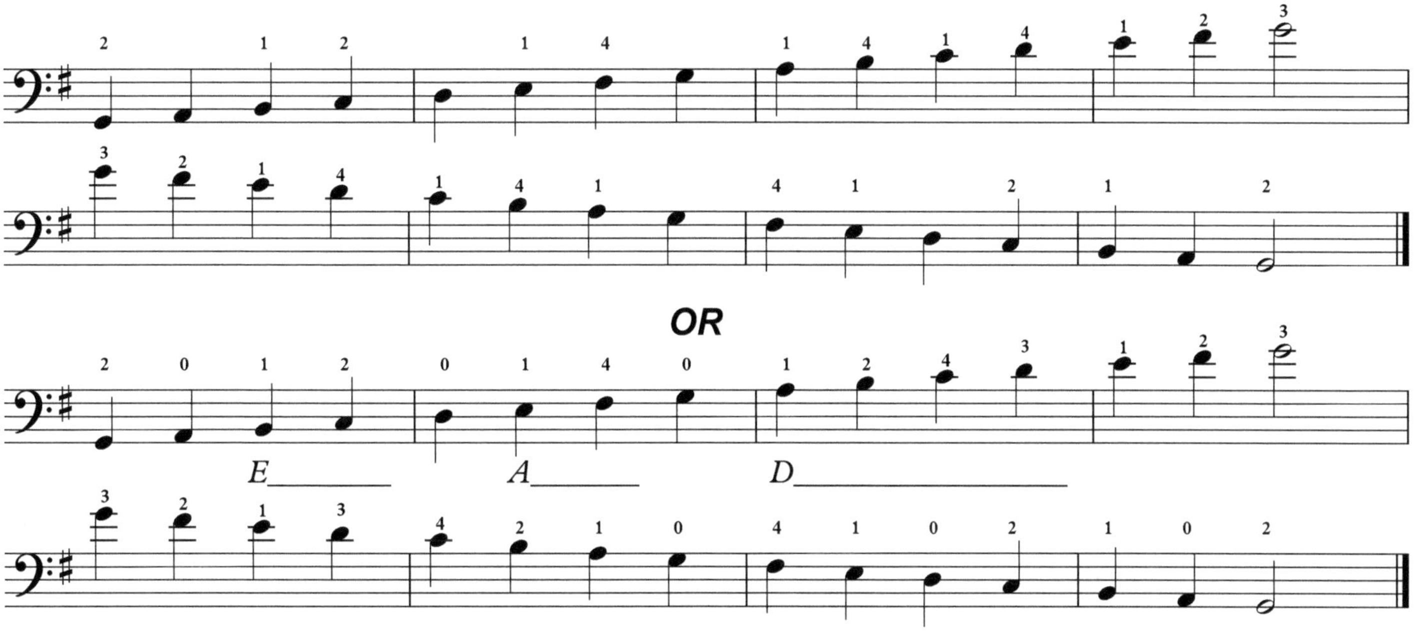

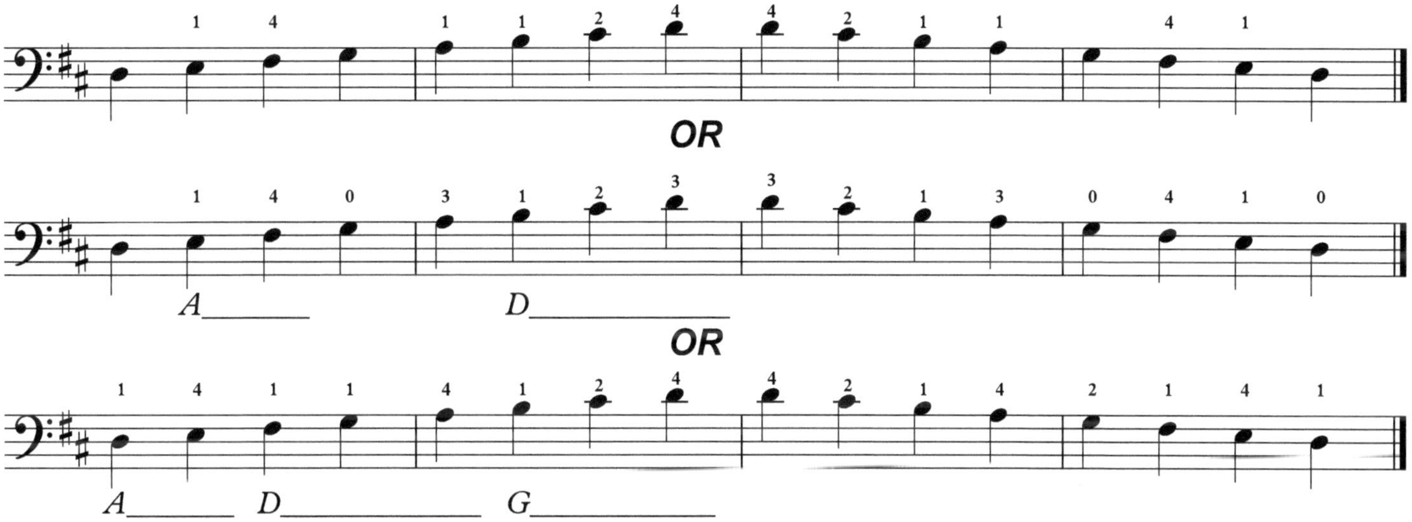

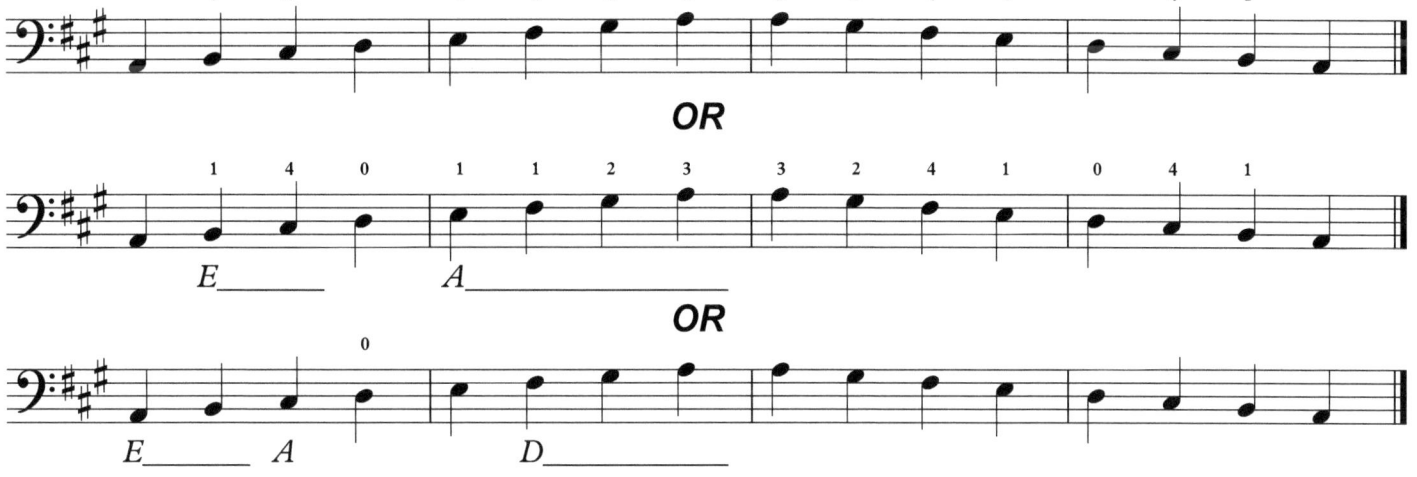

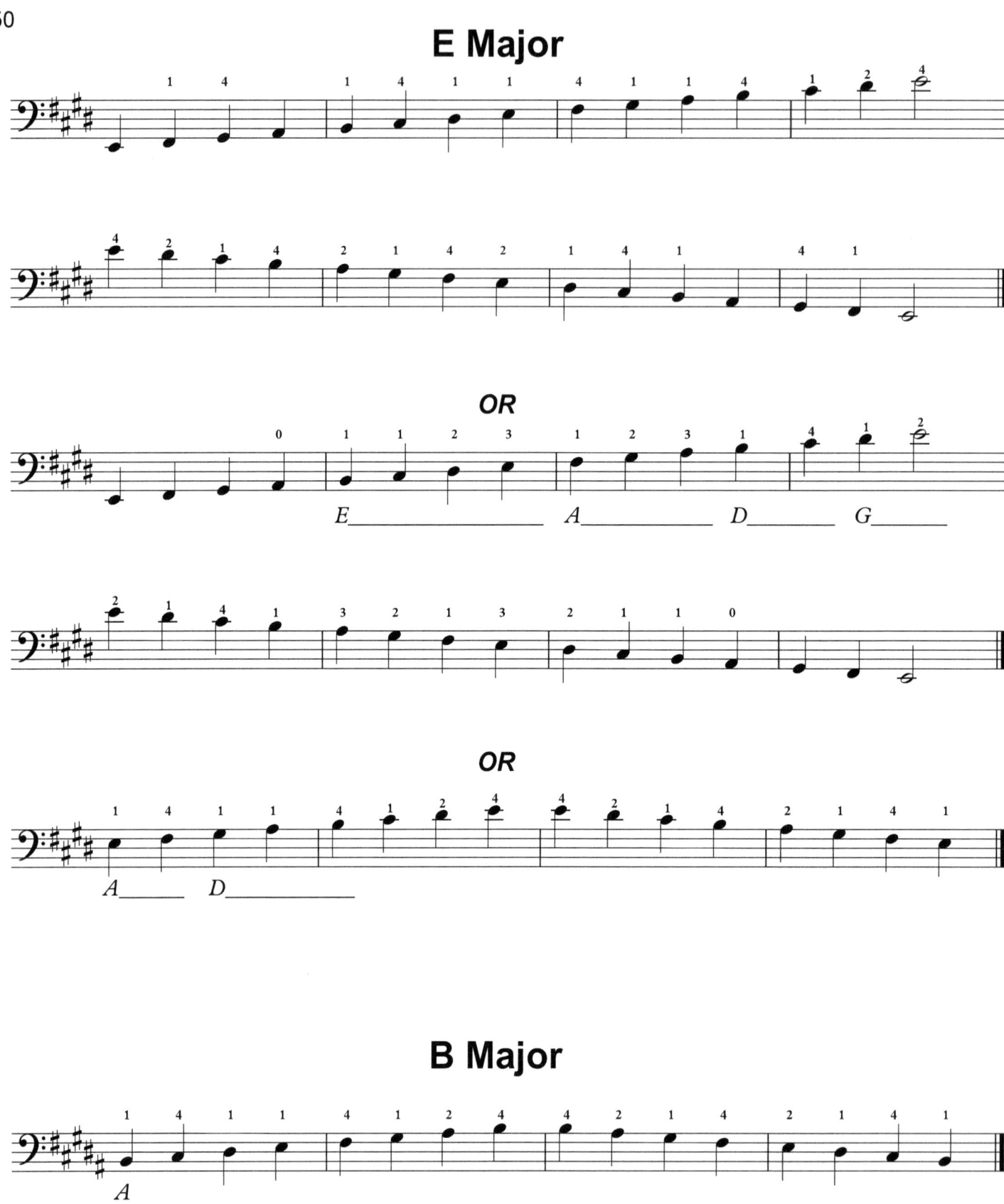

F# Major

OR

C# Major

OR

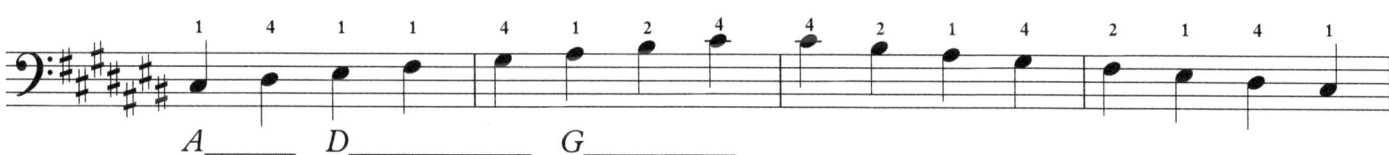

OR

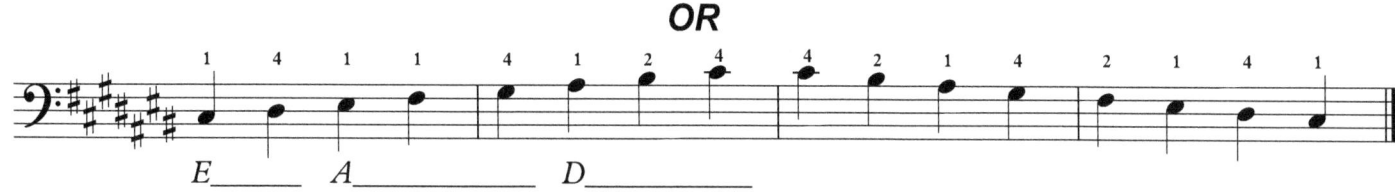

Horizontal Technique

The following sets of scales employ what I call the Horizontal Technique: the scales are played across the instrument, horizontally, rather than up and down, vertically. The same practice principles used in the preceding scales are used in these exercises.

Arpeggios

Arpeggios are a most important part of the development of one's technique. They aid in the developing of better pitch and tone, and, as I have fingered them in the following pages, increased facility.

You will notice that only the first four measures are fingered. With Horizontal Technique, the remaining measures use the same fingering. Follow the preceding sequence.

Again, I recommend that these arpeggios be practiced with much patience and much care.

Arpeggios

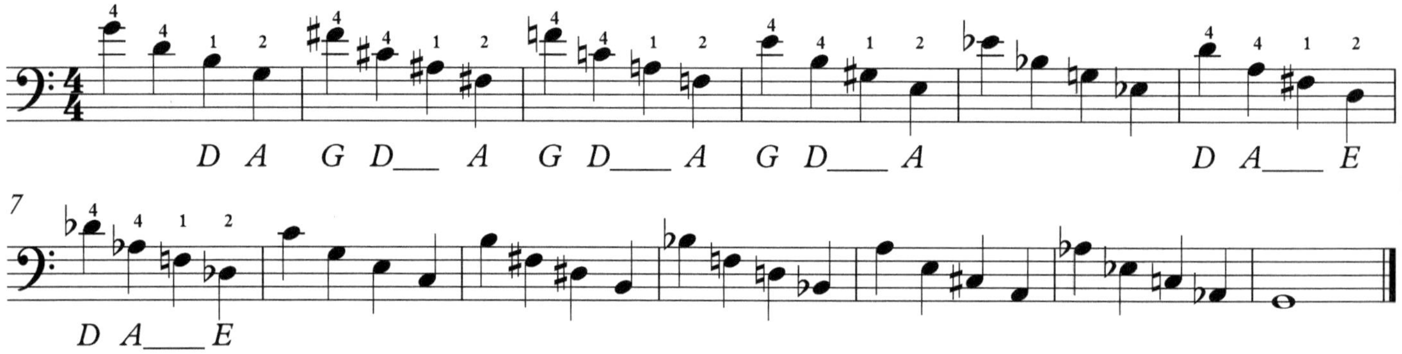

Arpeggios

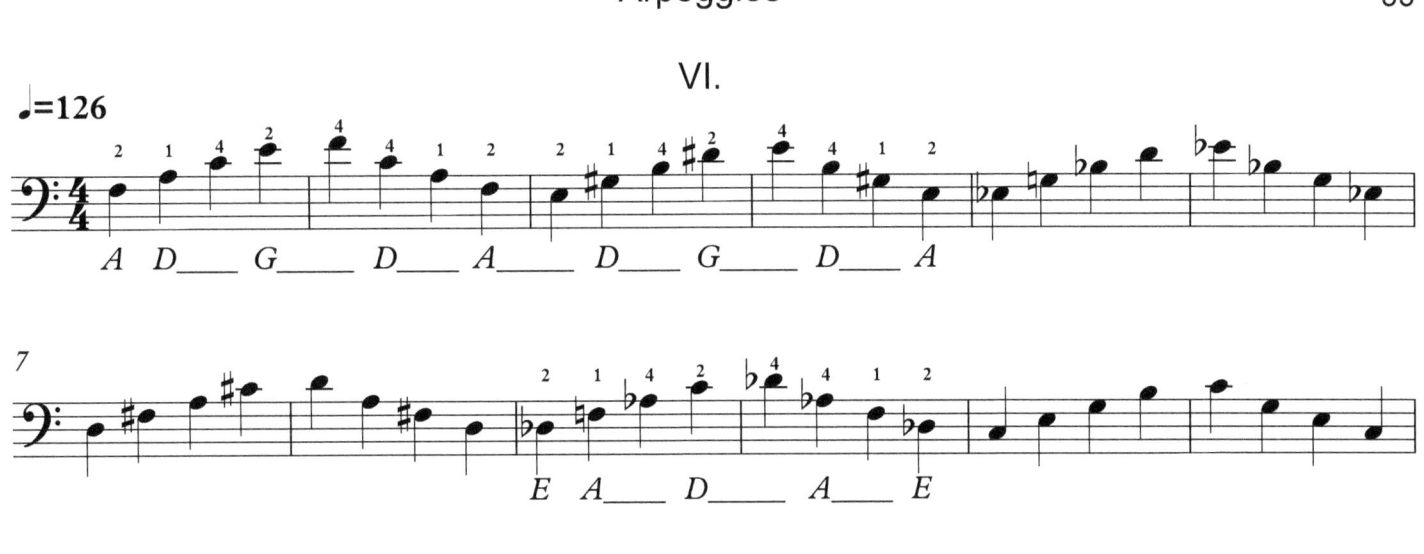

Arpeggios

VIII.

IX.
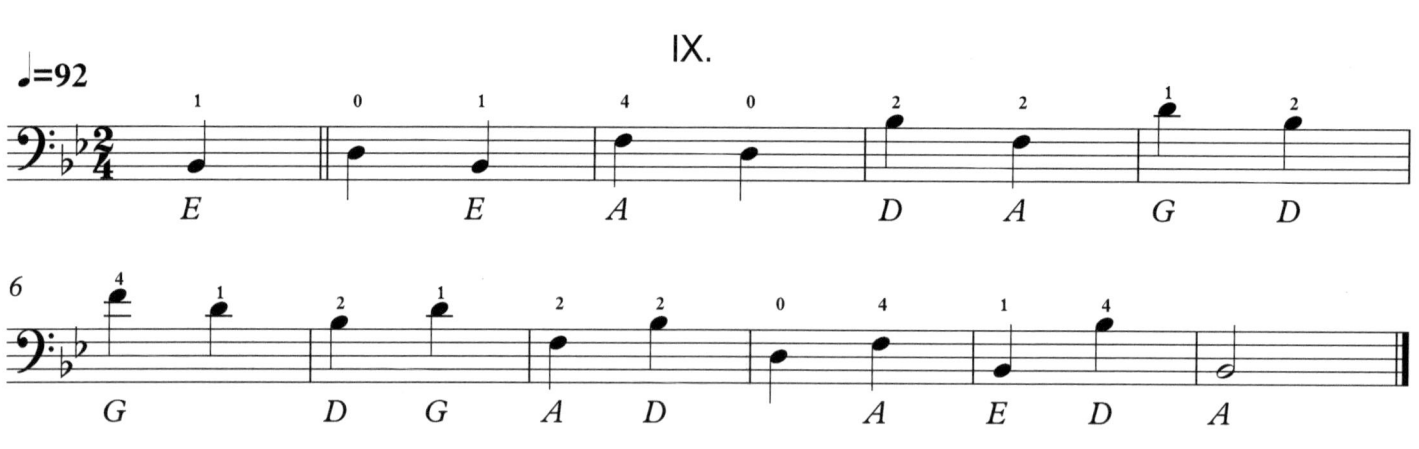

X.
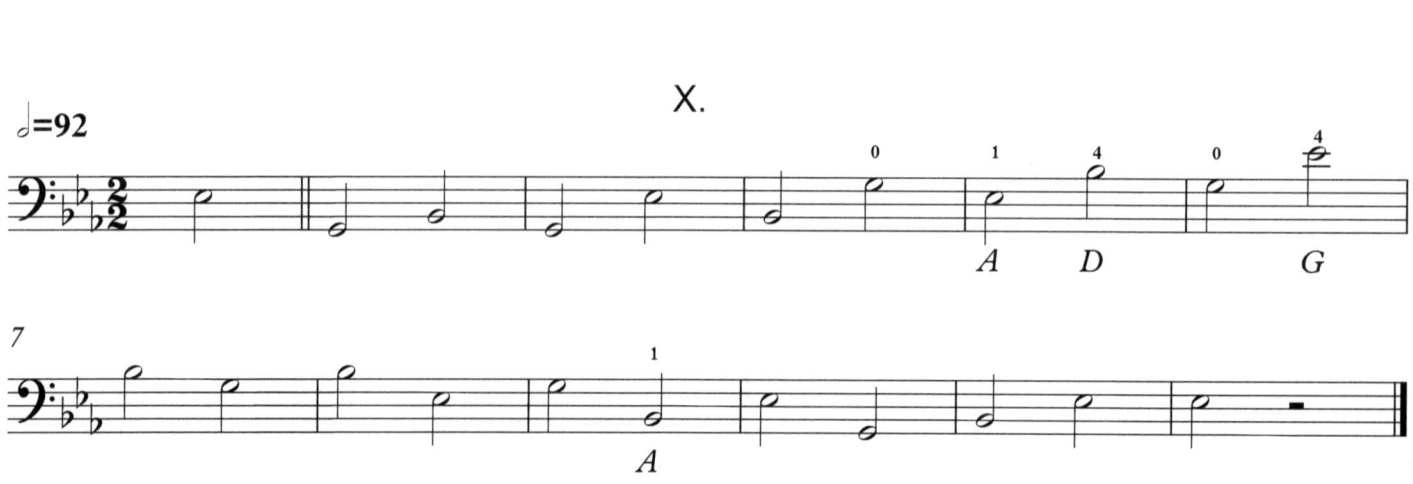

Arpeggios

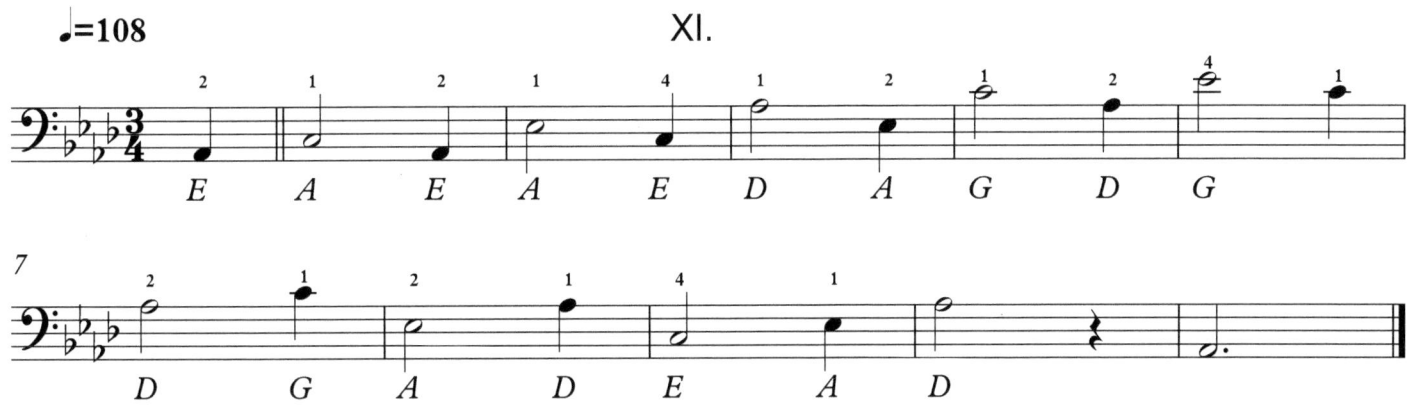

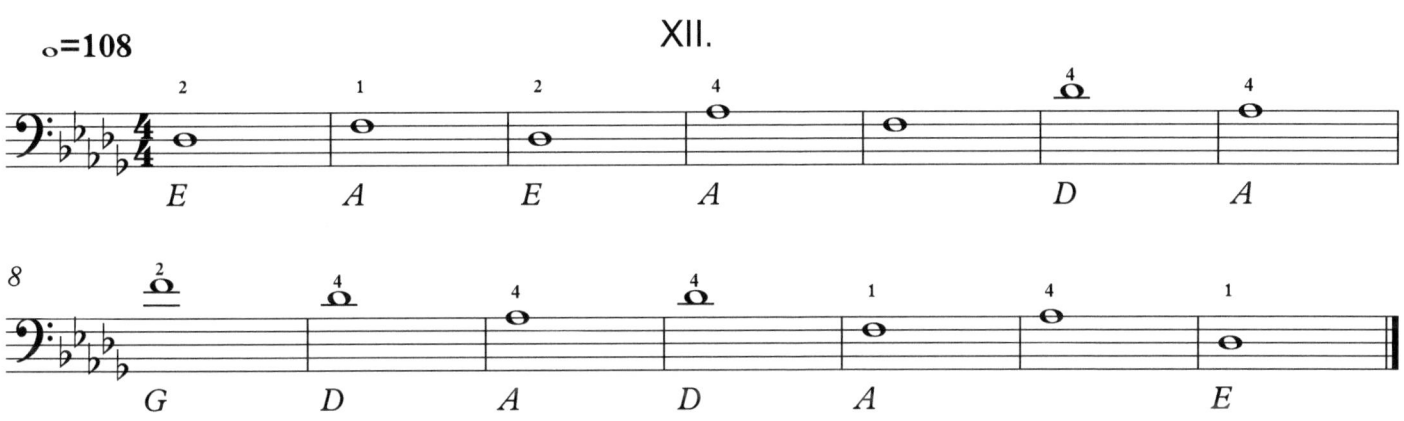

Arpeggios

XIV.
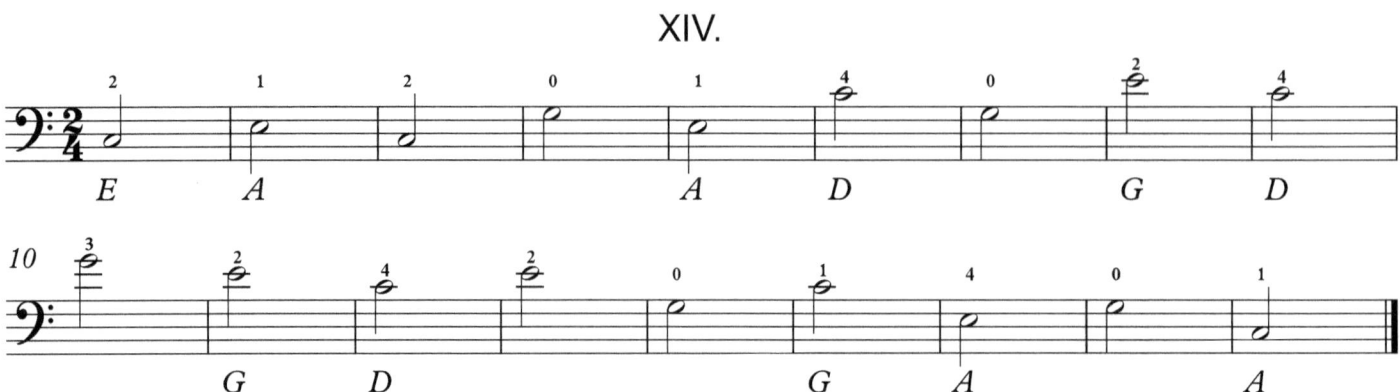

XV.
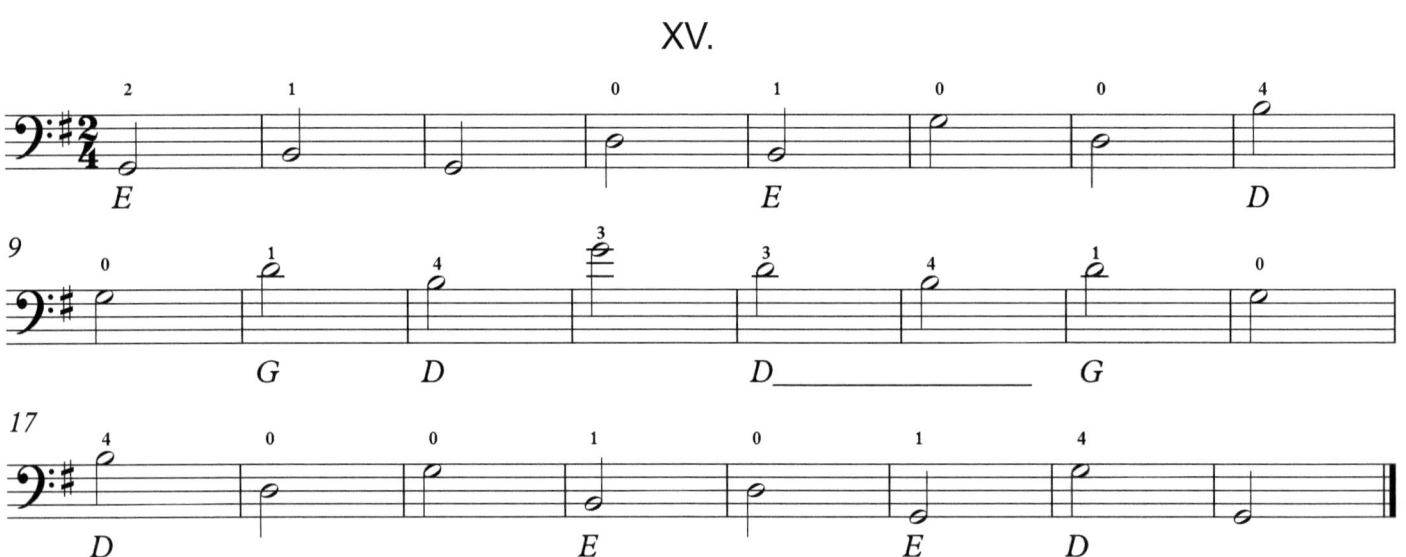

XVI.
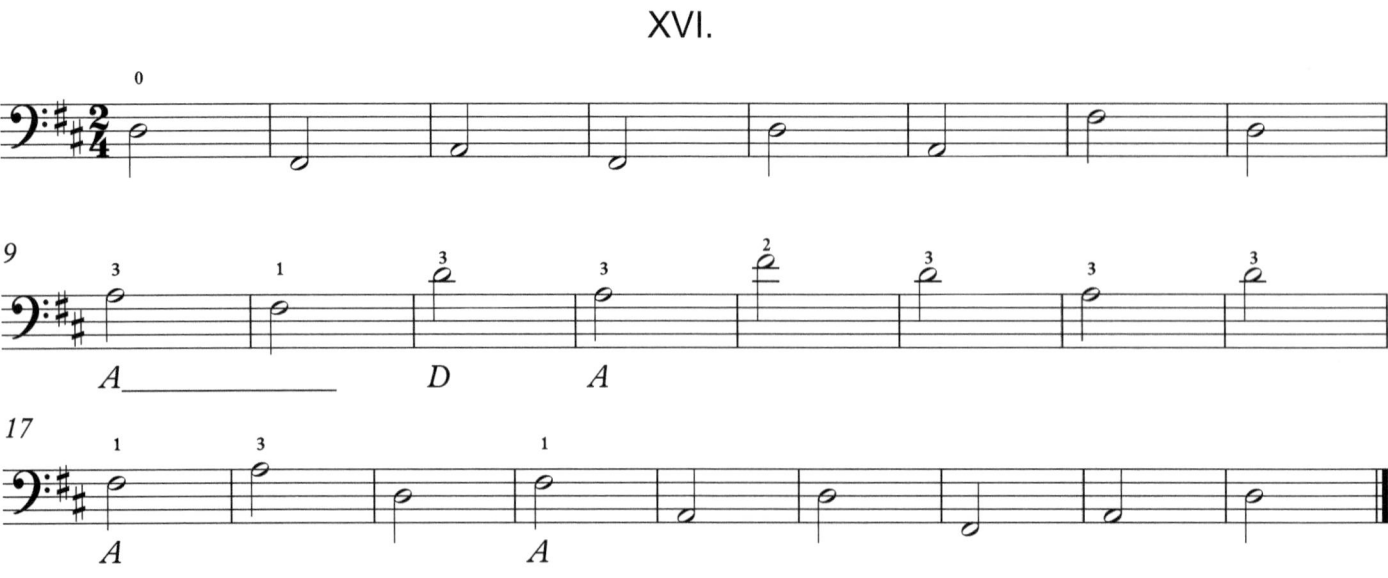

Arpeggios

XVII.

XVIII.

XIX.
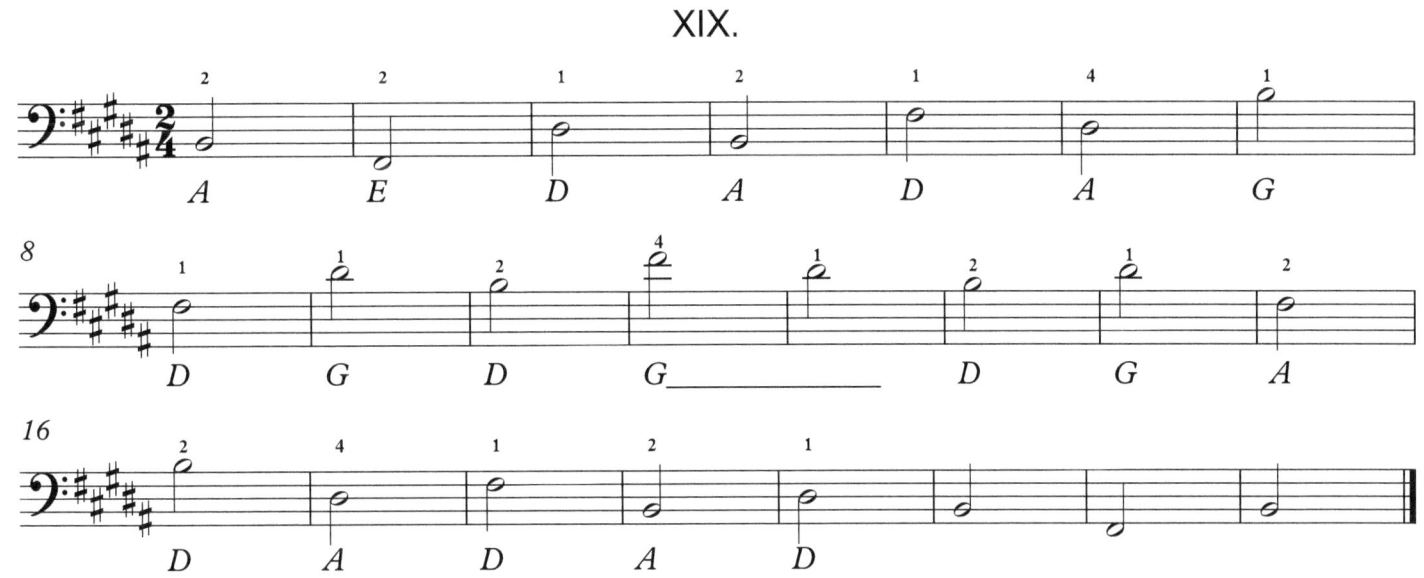

Blues in the Closet
from Ron Carter's "Stardust"

Ron Carter bass solo

For Toddlers Only

Leadsheet

Ron Carter

Receipt, Please

Ron Carter

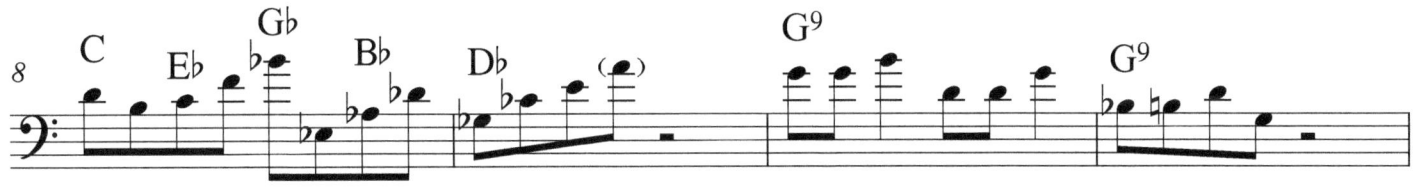

PLAYING TIP NO. 1: TIPS FOR PLAYERS

Ron, in his own words, from *Bass Player* magazine:

1. Find a teacher. Period.

2. Don't watch the piano player's left hand. Piano players often tell bassists, "Watch my left hand. The note I play with my left little finger is often the root of the chord." But that's not always the case; good piano players don't always play the root. They may play the third, or they may play no chord at all. To get a sound like Horace Silver or McCoy Tyner, the chord's sound and rhythm are what's important. If you rely on being visual to figure out what the chord is, you miss the point of hearing the music. You have to be able to hear the chords; you can't rely on the piano player's left hand to bail you out.

3. Learn some keyboard. Bass players should know what the chords look like on piano. That gives you an idea of how your bass note affects the quality of the sound—whether you play a C or a B-flat under a C7 chord, for example. If you have some keyboard skill, you can hear what that stuff sounds like. It also helps when you're learning a new tune; if you can get to a piano and figure out what the chords are, you can stumble through the melody.

4. Play as often as you can. The more you play, the more you can make mistakes and learn how to fix them. Don't limit yourself to one band and one concept of rhythm-section playing. The more experiences you have, the more you can bring it all under one umbrella.

5. Always know what your bass really sounds like. Go into a corner and play some scales, without trying to knock down the walls— you'll hear what kind of quality you actually have in that small space. Is the sound dark or light? Are the notes short, or are they long? Is the sound warm? Is it flat? Is there any resonance? I still do that because I want to know what happened last week - maybe the bass wasn't standing up straight enough, maybe the angle was too great or maybe my hands were too high. I just like to get an idea of what's going on with my bass and its sound.

Source: *Bass Player* magazine, September 2003, as told to feature writer Brigid Bergen. Used by permission of Brigid Bergen and *Bass Player*.

PLAYING TIP NO. 2: IMPROVISATION

Ron, in his own words, from *Strings* magazine:

1. The first thing any improviser must know is what chords are attached to each note. Classical players tend to saw away at notes or scrape the bow or pluck at random. They don't think about chords. They don't think to analyze. That's not the job of a second violinist in an orchestra. Knowing what the chords are is not their concern.

2. Our concern as jazz improvisers is much more complicated than just playing a note. You need to know what chords are attached to this note and what other chords can be used to give harmonic validity.

3. So, the first thing I'd suggest is learn harmony and theory to understand what chords do to certain melodies. Second, stay away from trying to play a lot of notes. Half notes are fabulous. Half notes and rests are two of the greatest things invented.

4. Improvising doesn't mean you have to have a different technique or skill. Jazz requires the same skill level as classical music, but it's more complicated because you play notes that you don't know are coming in advance. It's hard to prepare your left and right hands so as to make those notes easily attainable.

5. I'd recommend listening to as many jazz musicians as possible who play an instrument different from your own. A violin player could listen to Charlie Parker on saxophone or Miles Davis on trumpet. A cellist could listen to bassist Oscar Pettiford or me. By listening to others, you can get some ideas about how you could sound on your own instrument. For example, if you're a violinist and you listen to Jean-Luc Ponty, you may not learn what your own violin playing could be. That's what Ponty has done. Why not listen to a saxophone player to hear what other choices are available?

6. Last, don't worry about trying. You can't learn to improvise in three weeks. You can just keep working at it, and it'll come.

Source: *Strings Magazine* cover-story, Ron Carter: Dean of Jazz Bass," May 2004, issue number 119, as told to Dan Ouellette. © 2004 String Letter Publishing. Used by permission.

Photo: Seda Ozguven

Awards:

Grammy Awards: In 2022 Carter won with "Skyline" for Best Instrumental Jazz Album. In 1993, he earned a Grammy award for Best Jazz Instrumental Group, the Miles Davis Tribute Band and another Grammy in 1998 for "Call Sheet Blues", an instrumental composition from the film, Round Midnight.

International Awards: In 2021 the Japanese government awarded him The Order of the Rising Sun, Gold Rays with Rosette for his contributions to Japan-US relations in the field of music. In 2010 Carter was honored by the French Minister of Culture with France's premier cultural award, the medallion and title of Commander of the Order of Arts and Letters, given to those who have distinguished themselves in the domain of artistic or literary creation and for their contribution to the spread of arts and letters in France and the world.

Guinness World Record: In 2015 Carter earned a Guinness World Record as the most recorded jazz bassist with 2,221 recordings. Since that time he has recorded hundreds more.

Press Awards: Ron Carter was named "Outstanding Bassist of the Decade" by the Detroit News, Jazz Bassist of the Year by Downbeat magazine, and Most Valuable Player by the National Academy of Recording Arts and Sciences several times.

Education Awards: Carter earned seven honorary doctorates, Manhattan School of Music (1998), from the New England Conservatory of Music (1999), Berklee (2005), University of Rochester (2010), University of Michigan, (2016), Juilliard (2018) and Clark University 2023.

He was the 2002 recipient of the prestigious Hutchinson Award from the Eastman School at the University of Rochester

In 2021 he received the Satchmo Award from the Louis Armstrong Foundation for his lasting contribution to jazz as an educator.

BIOGRAPHY

RON CARTER is among the most original, prolific and influential bassists in jazz. He has recorded over 2200 albums and has a Guinness World Record to prove it!

In Jazz: From 1963 to 1968 he was a member of the acclaimed Miles Davis Quintet. He can be heard on many iconic jazz records of the 60's and 70's such as Speak No Evil, Maiden Voyage, Red Clay, Speak Like a Child, Nefertiti and Miles Smiles, to name a few.

In other music genres: After leaving the quintet he embarked on a prolific 60-year free-lance career that spanned vastly different music genres and continues to this day. He recorded with Roberta Flack, Billy Joel, Bette Midler, Paul Simon and Aretha Franklin, appeared on the seminal hip-hop album Low End Theory with A Tribe Called Quest, wrote and recorded pieces for string quartets and Bach chorales for 2-6 bassists and accompanied Danny Simmons on a spoken word album.

As a leader: Carter continues to do worldwide tours with his various groups, The Foursight Quartet, The Golden Striker Trio, Ron Carter's Great Big Band and the Ron Carter Nonet. He has recorded multiple albums with his groups.

As an author: Carter shares his expertise in the series of books he has authored, in which he explains his creative process and teaches bassists to improve their skills and develop their own unique sound. His books share a unique feature he pioneered, that of including QR codes in every book that lead to additional material, enriching the next and making each book that much more valuable.

In 2015 he penned his autobiography "Finding the Right Notes" which is available in print and e-book and also as an audio book read by the Maestro himself.

In 2021 Carter pioneered a new type of music transcription with "Chartography", which follows the development of the bass line for Autumn Leaves over 5 performances with the Miles Davis Quintet, showing not only the bass line but also how the band responded to it and how the entire tune transformed over time.

As a teacher: Carter has lectured, conducted and performed at clinics and master classes, instructing jazz ensembles and teaching the business of music at numerous universities. He was Artistic Director of the Thelonious Monk Institute of Jazz Studies when it was located in Boston and after 18 years on the faculty of the Music Department of the City College of New York he is now Distinguished Professor Emeritus. He also taught at the Julliard School and and at Manhattan School of Music.

In film scoring: In addition to scoring and arranging music for many films, including some projects for the Public Broadcasting System, Carter composed music for "A Gathering of Old Men" starring Lou Gosset Jr., "The Passion of Beatrice" directed by Bertrand Tavernier, and "Blind Faith" starring Courtney B. Vance

Film Appearances: In October 2022 PBS released a full-length feature film documentary on the Maestro's life called Ron Carter: Finding the Right Notes. Many jazz documentaries feature the Maestro because of his indelible contribution to the genre including Ken Burns' "Jazz", "Birth of the Cool" about Miles Davis, "It Must Be Schwing", the story of the Blue Note and many more. He also appeared as himself in HBO's hit series "Treme" and was the bassist on the soundtrack of "Twin Peaks", "Bird" and way too many others to mention.

THE COMPLETE RON CARTER LIBRARY

Transcriptions

Carter-isms: The Evolution of Bossa Nova Bass Lines from their origin in Brazil, to the New York Bossa sound that Carter created and continues to evolve today.

Chartography: Ron Carter's original, unique re-invention of transcriptions and their study. Transcriptions of the bass lines from 5 performances of Autumn Leaves by the Miles Davis Quintet. A detailed chart of how the bass line evolved and how the band responded. Includes QR codes to audio of each performance transcribed. Also available in Japanese.

The Art of Ron Carter 1963-1968 By Mikko Nurmi. Precise, accurate transcriptions of his bass lines and explanations of how and why they worked so well. 230 pages, a professional, literary presentation for all jazz bass historians and jazz bassists.

9 Transcriptions Every bassist should study

Books

Bass Drops: 30 Examples of Non-Quarter Note Bass Line Rhythms All Levels

Mix & Match: Advanced Guide to Creating Great Bass Lines. With "Dutch Door" pages to mix and match choruses and bass lines.

Comprehensive Bass Method Advanced Level: Shows bassists how to master pizzicato and horizontal technique. Also available in Japanese and Portuguese.

Behind the Changes: Intermediate guide to how to change the changes with each chorus. Transparent overlay pages Also available in Portuguese.

Blueprint for the Working Jazz Bassist: Intermediate guide to creating your own unique sound.

The Ron Carter Songbook: Includes Little Waltz, Eighty-One and 131 more Ron Carter compositions. Available in treble and bass clef.

Finding the Right Notes: Ron Carter's iconic autobiography. Available in paperback and e-book. Audio book, read by the Maestro himself,

From the Bottom Up: Creativity and Individuality in Jazz. Interviews with 7 legendary bassists. By Gui Duvigneau.

Scores and Parts

Scores and Parts for string ensembles: Arrangements of 4 Carter compositions:

2+1=4 for violin, viola and cello
Desert Winds and Loose Change each for 4 cellos
Serenade for viola and 4 cellos

Ron Carter Meets Bach: Scores and parts for 13 Bach chorales for 2-8 basses. Arranged by Ron Carter. Available in 3 volumes

Big Band Scores – 10 Ron Carter Compositions arranged by Rich DeRosa

Big Band Scores – 10 Jazz Standards plus 2 Ron Carter tunes arranged by Bob Freedman

Available exclusively at www.roncarterjazz.com